GRADUATION *for* ALL

GRADUATION *for* ALL

A Practical Guide to Decreasing School Dropout

Camilla A. Lehr
Ann T. Clapper
Martha L. Thurlow

CORWIN PRESS
A SAGE Publications Company
Thousand Oaks, California

For information:

Corwin Press
A Sage Publications Company
2455 Teller Road
Thousand Oaks, California 91320
www.corwinpress.com

Sage Publications Ltd.
1 Oliver's Yard
55 City Road
London EC1Y 1SP
United Kingdom

Sage Publications India Pvt. Ltd.
B-42, Panchsheel Enclave
Post Box 4109
New Delhi 110 017 India

Printed in the United States of America.

Library of Congress Cataloging-in-Publication Data

Lehr, Camilla A. Graduation for all: A practical guide to decreasing school
dropout / Camilla A. Lehr, Ann T. Clapper, Martha L. Thurlow.
      p. cm.
Includes bibliographical references and index.
ISBN 1-4129-0626-1 (cloth)
ISBN 1-4129-0627-X (pbk.)
    1. Dropouts—United Statess—Prevention. 2. School improvement programs—United States.
3. Educational change—United States. I. Clapper, Ann T. II. Thurlow, Martha L. III.   Title.
LC143.L45 2005
373.12'913—dc22

                                2004030485

This book is printed on acid-free paper.

05   06   07   08   09   10   9   8   7   6   5   4   3   2   1

Acquisitions Editor:	Elizabeth Brenkus
Editorial Assistants:	Candice L. Ling and Jingle Vea
Production Editor:	Denise Santoyo
Copy Editor:	Pam Suwinsky
Typesetter:	C&M Digitals (P) Ltd.
Indexer:	Sylvia Coates
Cover Designer:	Michael Dubowe
Graphic Designer:	Lisa Miller

Contents

Preface

Every day there are students who leave school before they graduate—never to return. Others leave and then come back, eventually completing school, but in a less than efficient and satisfying manner. Failure to graduate—dropping out—is a problem that has been around for many years. It has been a blip on the radar screen, emerging only every so often as people become concerned about whether our country is losing valuable resources when students do not complete school.

Perhaps more than ever before, the current context of educational reform in the United States has alerted the country to the importance of having all students graduate from high school with a diploma. This press toward "graduation for all" has to do with wanting an educated citizenry—one that contributes to, rather than burdens, our economy.

Recent federal legislation has focused attention on the problem of too many students dropping out of school and is a driving force in efforts to increase the rate of graduation for all students. The No Child Left Behind Act (NCLB) holds schools accountable for student progress using indicators of adequate yearly progress (AYP) that include not only measures of academic performance but also graduation rates. Employers today are no longer willing to hire youth who do not have the skills that they are supposed to learn in high school. And, society cannot afford to support the costs of lost revenue, welfare, unemployment, crime prevention, criminal proceedings, and incarceration often associated with students who drop out of school.

We wrote this book with the desire to provide information that will help reach the goal of graduation for all. We have developed a practical guide that we believe will aid in decreasing the rate of school dropouts, and at the same time increase the graduation rate.

AUDIENCE

Educators, administrators, and policymakers at district and state levels are on the front line in the fight to promote graduation for all. We have written this book to be a resource to all district and school professionals developing prevention and intervention programs to decrease dropout and increase graduation. The book is also appropriate for teams of individuals that may include principals, teachers, counselors, school psychologists, curriculum specialists, attendance coordinators, directors of special services, educators and coordinators of alternative schools, and assistant superintendents and superintendents.

We believe that the book also will be useful to several other audiences. For example, teachers-in-training will gain much from this book because working with students at risk is part of the job. Similarly, we believe that it will be of benefit to personnel from state-level education agencies who assist with and facilitate the development and implementation of systemic interventions that will effectively improve graduation rates. Other professionals who work with school, district, and state-level teams also will benefit from this book, including, for example, court liaisons, community agency personnel (YMCA, mental health clinics, organizations focused on pregnancy and parenting), and other business organizations (those that may assist with service learning projects or mentoring projects). The book also is useful for parents and parent organizations seeking to determine what schools can do for their children.

OVERVIEW

We have organized this book to give you both the information that you need to understand the topic and the tools that you need to take action. In each chapter, readers are provided with both "knowing" and "doing" information. Reflection Questions in each chapter are provided to help you think deeply about some of the knowledge information that is provided. But, because the dropout problem is not just something to be admired, this book is rich in tools—tools that you can use to help you take action to deal with the dropout problem in the context of your own school, your child's school, or a school you will be in someday. These are Action Tools.

Each chapter is organized in a way that makes it easy for you to attend to information that is important to you—advanced organizers that list the topics in the chapter and the things that you will learn from the chapter—as well as a Summary to provide a quick review of the main points in the chapter. Further Reading is provided with each chapter, which includes key references as well as sources of additional information and additional readings should you want to dig deeper than was possible in the chapter in this book.

Finally, we have included three key appendices. One is a Directory of Action Tools that allows you to see a listing of them at a glance in one place. Another is a Selected Glossary of terms—those terms that are used in this book and that everyone should use in the same way. The third, Related Links, is a list of Web sites and other resources that address dropout prevention and closely related topics.

We believe that we have developed a book that will help you attack the dropout problem. We firmly believe that to do so, you need both information and tools with which to work. We have provided these for you here. We hope that as you use this book, you will provide us with feedback on its usefulness in addressing the dropout problem and in increasing graduation for all in your school or district.

ACKNOWLEDGMENTS

This book is based on the accumulated knowledge of years of research and practice at the University of Minnesota and schools throughout this state and elsewhere. We could not have completed this book without the influence of many people and events. We are particularly grateful for the support of our colleagues, Sandra

Christenson and David Johnson, who encouraged the three of us to prepare a book that would speak to practitioners and provide them with tools to reach the goal of graduation for all. We would like to acknowledge the expertise of these two individuals, as well as another colleague, Mary Sinclair, and others, who have shaped our thinking on the issue of dropout in the past and currently.

We also owe a debt of gratitude to the many individuals who spoke to us over the phone and in person about their district and state approaches to dropout prevention—about what things were and were not working, and about what the major issues were that needed to be addressed. There are too many people to list, but we want all to know that in some way or another, all of their comments were mulled over, thought about, digested, and reflected in this book.

There are several individuals whose help we want specifically to acknowledge. First, we would like to thank Sylvie Hale at WestEd for allowing us to model the Action Tools in this book on a format used in her book on comprehensive school reform. Lori Anderson assisted with formatting many of the tools with quick turnaround and helpful suggestions. Two key staff from the Minneapolis Public Schools reviewed and provided feedback on many of the tools to make sure that they were workable in the school setting. These individuals included Mary Barrie and Michael Luseni. To each of these individuals we owe a large debt of gratitude.

In addition, we would like to thank several individuals who reviewed the book. The valuable contributions and thoughtful comments of the following reviewers were greatly appreciated.

Elaine Allensworth, Associate Director, Consortium on Chicago School Research
University of Chicago, Chicago, IL

Nancy Avolese, State Coordinator, Alternative Education for Disruptive Youth
Pennsylvania Department of Education, Harrisburg, PA

Everett Bad Wound, Educational Specialist
Bureau of Indian Affairs, Arlington, VA

Victoria Bernhardt, Executive Director, Author
Education for the Future, California State University, Chico, CA

Russell Dever, Superintendent
Town of Barnstable Public Schools, Linwood, NJ

Judy Elliott, Director of Special Education
Long Beach Unified School District, Long Beach, CA

Carol Grant-Watt, Principal
Bert Church High School, Airdrie, AB, Canada

Jay Greene, Senior Fellow
Manhattan Institute for Policy Research, Weston, FL

Robert McCauley, Secondary Academic Superintendent
Minneapolis Public Schools, Minneapolis, MN

Gerry Olvey, Program Specialist
Mountain Plains Regional Resource Center, North Logan, UT

Russell Rumberger, Professor, Gevirtz Graduate School of Education
University of California, Santa Barbara, CA

Frank Schargel, Senior Managing Associate
School Success Network, Albuquerque, NM

Jay Smink, Executive Director, Author
National Dropout Prevention Center, Clemson University, Clemson, SC

We hope that the approval reflected by the reviewers carries over to you the reader. That is our true goal—to meet your needs, and in meeting your needs to have an impact on the dropout rate and, in turn, to strive toward graduation for all in our schools.

Camilla A. Lehr
Ann T. Clapper
Martha L. Thurlow

About the Authors

Camilla A. Lehr, PhD, is Research Associate with the Institute on Community Integration (University Center for Excellence in Developmental Disabilities) at the University of Minnesota. She is the Principal Investigator and Director of the Alternative Schools Research Project, a three-year federally funded project studying alternative schools across the nation and the role they play in preventing dropout, providing quality education for students at risk, and serving students with disabilities. Prior to directing the Alternative Schools Research Project, she co-directed a truancy prevention/student engagement project for children and youth in elementary and middle schools (Check & Connect). She has held interim and adjunct faculty positions at the University of Minnesota (School Psychology Program) and at Hamline University (Education Department) respectively. Prior to returning to the university in 1988, Lehr worked as a licensed school psychologist in a large suburban school district. She has worked in the educational arena for nearly 20 years. Her research interests are focused in the areas of dropout prevention, engaging children and youth placed at risk in school, and promoting positive school climates. She is lead author on several recent products in the area of dropout prevention, including an integrative review of interventions focused on dropout described in the professional literature, and an *Essential Tools Manual, Increasing Rates of School Completion: Moving from Policy and Research to Practice,* published by the National Center on Secondary Education and Transition. Lehr has presented at a variety of local and national conferences. She has coauthored research reports, journal articles, book chapters, and other documents with national impact.

Ann T. Clapper, EdD, is Research Associate at the National Center on Educational Outcomes (NCEO) in the Institute on Community Integration (University Center for Excellence in Developmental Disabilities) at the University of Minnesota. Her current projects include researching state policies on accommodations and designing self-assessment tools on the use of accommodations during instruction and on assessments for students with disabilities. As an associate director for a related ICI project, the National Center on Secondary Education and Transition (NCSET), Clapper provided training for secondary school principals on creating effective learning environments for students with disabilities. Topics for articles she has coauthored include adolescent literacy, universal design for learning, teacher quality, and accommodations policies and practices. Prior to joining NCEO, she served as the Director of Curriculum Leadership and Improvement for the North Dakota Department of Public Instruction. Her work there involved coordinating the design and implementation of the state content standards, providing technical assistance to districts on systemic school improvement, and designing practical tools to guide them in the process. Her 30 years of experience in education also include serving as an elementary and middle school teacher, a special education coordinator, a regional educational facilitator, and a college instructor.

 **Martha L. Thurlow, PhD,** is Director of the National Center on Educational Outcomes in the Institute on Community Integration (University Center for Excellence in Developmental Disabilities) at the University of Minnesota. In this position, she addresses the implications of contemporary U.S. policy and practice for students with disabilities and English Language Learners, including national and statewide assessment policies and practices, standards-setting efforts, and graduation requirements. Thurlow has conducted research for the past 35 years in a variety of areas, including assessment and decision making, learning disabilities, early childhood education, dropout prevention, effective classroom instruction, and integration of students with disabilities in general education settings. She has published extensively on all of these topics, and also recently completed serving as coeditor with Bob Algozzine of *Exceptional Children*, the research journal of the Council for Exceptional Children. Thurlow is a coauthor of several books, including *Testing Students With Disabilities, Improving Test Performance of Students With Disabilities, Alternate Assessments for Students With Disabilities,* and *Critical Issues in Special Education.* She was one of the original developers of the dropout prevention program Check & Connect, which was empirically tested and replicated in several settings. She is the author of numerous reports, journal articles, and chapters on the topic of dropouts and dropout prevention, and also addresses the dropout problem within the current context of federal legislation, high-stakes testing, and standards-based education.

To our children, Luke, Nicholas, Kiley, Lisa, and Rob

1

What This Book Is About

TOPICS

- Importance of Raising Graduation Rates
- Implications of Current Reform Context
- Critical Need for Knowing and Doing
- Overview of This Book

Never before has it seemed so important to our country that all students graduate from high school with the knowledge and skills to meet the demands of the workplace and of society as a whole. A diploma is the most commonly accepted document indicating successful completion of high school. The press for an educated citizenry is the result of many factors, driven in large part by economic factors. But, it is not just the importance of graduation rates to our country that has pushed us to write this book. It is the importance of graduation to the youth of our country in the early 21st century who find too many doors closed to them—regardless of their knowledge or skills—when they do not have that simple piece of paper: the high school diploma.

In this chapter, we provide a brief overview of the importance of raising graduation rates and the cost of students dropping out of school. We also highlight the implications of the current education reform context, and specifically the No Child Left Behind (NCLB) Act, for graduation rate calculations. Finally, we talk turkey—what is the purpose of this book? How have we organized it to make it most useful for you as you use it?

One of the techniques that we use in our chapters throughout the book to help focus your reading is to identify topic-specific myths and truths. Test your knowledge now, then check yourself when you finish reading the chapter. The Myth or Truth? statements appear in boxes at the beginning of each chapter; for Chapter 1 they are presented in Box 1.1. The answers appear in a similar box at the end of the chapter.

Box 1.1 Myth or Truth? Do You Know?

Read each statement following and decide whether it is a myth or the truth.

1. Those who drop out of school are more likely to be unemployed.

2. Dropouts tend to create significant costs to society.

3. Most states met the goal of a 90% school completion rate in the year 2000.

4. The percentage of students graduating from high school is an adequate yearly progress accountability indicator.

5. The No Child Left Behind Act requires graduation exams.

IMPORTANCE OF RAISING GRADUATION RATES

High school graduation rates have grown dramatically from the early 1900s, when 96% of all individuals 18 years and older had not completed high school. By the 1960s, the noncompletion rate was only about one-fourth of this population, and today it is closer to 14% of all youth. That is a lot of improvement! So, why are we concerned about raising graduation rates?

There are three main reasons that we are concerned and need to be concerned about raising graduation rates and decreasing school dropouts: (1) extensiveness of the issue, (2) costs to the individual, and (3) costs to society. We discuss each of these briefly here. In Chapter 3, we devote a little more attention to the numbers and what they mean in general and for your own context.

Extensiveness of the Issue

School dropouts are easily hidden in statistics, even when they are a huge issue. We have used the term *extensive* here because we believe that the school dropout issue is extensive, even though it is not necessarily always evident how extensive it is.

In 2002, the National Center for Education Statistics indicated that hundreds of thousands of students in the United States leave school early each year without successfully completing school. A study by Jay Greene and others at the Manhatten Institute for Policy Research, highlighting variability in graduation rates across states, indicated that the percentage of eighth grade students who graduate five years later ranged from a low of 55% in Florida to a high of 87% in New Jersey.

There are many factors that come into play in these types of numbers. And, there are many other numbers that need to be investigated, including what the graduation and dropout rates look like for different subgroups of students, and whether the rates are influenced when certain types of exit documents (certificates of attendance, General Educational Development—GED—diplomas, or Individualized Educational Program—IEP—diplomas) are not counted in graduation rates. For now, suffice it to say that there is a fair amount of evidence—and more that we look at in Chapter 3—to indicate that we have a problem that needs to be addressed. This book is designed to address it where we can do that best: at the district and school levels.

Costs to the Individual

Dropping out of school rarely is a good thing, especially in today's world. There are few employers willing even to consider hiring a person who does not have a high school diploma. Research has confirmed that those who drop out of school are more likely to be unemployed, or to have jobs that do not use the skills that they do have. School dropouts are found among the populations in jails and prisons more often than are those who graduated from high school.

All of these indicators are what the research calls costs to the individual. They are ways in which the individual "pays" for not having obtained the high school diploma. It is the rare individual who manages to get beyond the baggage of not having a high school diploma to end up in a successful and well-paying job. The one or two individuals who have done this are legends—the material of Hollywood films. It is a dangerous fallacy to believe that many individuals can pull themselves up from not having a high school diploma to become thriving and successful adults, especially in today's economic realities.

Costs to Society

While we can all understand costs to the individual and how significant they are, it is *costs to society* that drive the need for federal and state programs to raise graduation rates and decrease school dropouts. What do we mean by costs to society? Consider what happens when students graduate from high school. Most either obtain jobs or go on for additional education or training. These students are almost guaranteed higher paying jobs than those students who have dropped out of school.

Unless economic times are very good, and jobs are very plentiful, students who have dropped out of school tend to have a very difficult time finding jobs and are more likely to end up needing assistance from governmental agencies. They are less likely to pay taxes, and even if they pay taxes, they are likely to pay much less than they would have had they completed high school and obtained higher paying jobs. School dropouts are not giving to society what they could have, and therefore, they are costing society.

U.S. Census Bureau educational attainment by earnings figures for 2002 indicate that students who receive a high school diploma or GED diploma earn on average about $29,200, while those who exit school between Grades 9 and 12 without a diploma earn on average about $22,500. These figures, of course, change with the economic times. Researcher Jay Greene reported just a few years earlier that the 1999 Current Population Survey of the U.S. Census showed that those who earned a high school diploma or GED earned $29,294 compared to $15,334 for those without these diplomas. In a report titled *The Big Payoff*, the U.S. Census Bureau estimated that workers who were high school graduates earned about $270,000 more over their work lives than high school dropouts. These differences have significant implications for the tax dollars used for public services and societal benefits.

Our society depends on certain things to keep it running successfully. It depends on the collection of sufficient taxes and the minimal use of funds to support people who are not working or who have committed crimes. Youth who do not graduate from school and youth who drop out of school tend to create significant costs to society in the form of lost tax revenues, increased welfare and unemployment costs, and increased prosecution and incarceration costs. The specific costs that are created by dropouts are difficult to estimate because they do vary with the economic times. But clearly, the costs are too high.

IMPLICATIONS OF CURRENT REFORM CONTEXT

The current context of reform has been bubbling for years. It probably started most recently in 1983 when *A Nation at Risk* was published, declaring that the American education had lost its edge—once gained back after the Sputnik scare in the 1950s. In 1983, the National Commission on Excellence in Education found that the U.S. educational system was severely lacking in rigor, and that students who left school with diplomas did not have the skills that students in other nations had. States and districts reacted by increasing course and credit requirements, with apparently little effect on international test results. Then, all of the states' governors met in a national summit in 1989. At this summit, they identified a set of national education goals that became the basis for a law known as Goals 2000. One of the primary goals was that the high school graduation rate would be 90% by the year 2000.

Despite all this attention, including yearly reports that marked each state's progress and the nation's progress toward meeting each of the national education goals, only 17 states had achieved the 90% school completion rate by the year 2000. Note that slight change in wording from "graduation rate" to "completion rate." When the National Education Goals Panel defined the measures for Goal 2, "graduation rate" was changed to "school completion rate," so that graduation with an IEP diploma and a GED diploma were counted along with standard high school diplomas.

At the same time as Goals 2000 existed, the Elementary and Secondary Education Act (ESEA) of 1994 (called the Improving America's Schools Act) emphasized the importance of clear and rigorous content standards for all students. There was no mention of graduation standards in this law, but there was a firm and consistent message that all students should be held to high and rigorous standards, and that state assessments were to be the measure of the success of school programs in ensuring that all students reached high academic standards.

When Goals 2000 ended in the year 2000, with disappointing results on nearly all goals, and it was also time for the reauthorization of ESEA, the concern about graduation rates was reignited. Thus, when ESEA was reauthorized in 2001 as the No Child Left Behind Act, graduation rate became the "additional" accountability indicator (in addition to assessment results) at the high school level. When this happened, the interest in increasing graduation rates escalated considerably. In many states, NCLB added to already existing high-stakes tests that determined whether students earned standard diplomas.

No Child Left Behind Defined "Standard" Diploma

NCLB requires that schools and districts include the percentage of students graduating from high school as an accountability indicator at the high school level, contributing to the determination of whether adequate yearly progress was achieved. In other words, each year, the graduation rate had to increase steadily, reaching a "proficient" level by 2014.

How *graduation rate* is actually defined now becomes very important. Language in the law clearly indicates that the graduation rate includes only those students earning standard diplomas within four years of their ninth grade year in school, not those earning alternative graduation certificates such as GEDs. Any variation from this definition has to be explained in state accountability plans.

Narrow definitions of what constitutes "graduation" create several challenges for some subgroups of students, particularly students with disabilities and English language learners. We examine the definitional issues as we explore in a little more depth what we know about the dropout problem and its statistics in Chapter 3.

State High-Stakes Testing

NCLB and other federal legislation say nothing about requiring students to pass tests to earn a high school diploma. Instead, governors and state legislators in more than 25 states now have enacted laws that require students to pass tests to receive a standard diploma. In some states, a single test that covers a wide range of content must be passed, while in other states, tests in multiple content areas must be passed. More recently, states have begun to implement end-of-course testing as a graduation requirement, with certain courses and the passing of their tests required for the receipt of a standard diploma. In some states, there are alternative routes to earning the standard diploma that are available to some or all students in the state. What seems like it should be a very simple procedure—testing students to see whether they earn diplomas—is actually very complicated.

CRITICAL NEED FOR KNOWING AND DOING

As we developed this book, we realized that as readers, you need two critical things. First, you need to know certain things. Some of this is basic information, and some of it is scientifically based evidence about what works to address the dropout problem. Second, you need to know what to do—what actions to take—to prevent dropouts within the circle of your influence. We have attempted to meet both of these needs—the knowing needs and the doing needs—through the content and design of this book.

We have included strategies and approaches to the dropout problem that are based on research and scientific evidence. We try to make these as transparent as possible. We do not bog you down in the details of the research and scientific evidence, but try to give you pathways to them so that if you want to go there you can.

We have also included actions you can take. We have provided some things to do that help you make your way through the book—to help you process the content of the book, such as the Myth or Truth? boxes. And, we have provided some tools that help you dig into the context of the dropout problem in your school or your community. More on these "doing activities" is provided in the next section of the chapter.

OVERVIEW OF THIS BOOK

We know that you are busy, and that if you are reading this book it is because you are concerned about a real and important issue that faces youth and schools today. School dropout is not a simple problem with a simple solution. It requires a multifaceted

Figure 1.1 Organization of Book

Setting the Stage ❶

❷ Understanding the Problem and Possible Solutions

❸ Putting the Pieces Together

❹ Implementation and Evaluation

approach that addresses multiple challenges. But school dropout is an issue that can be addressed and systematically attacked so that we dramatically decrease school dropouts and move toward graduation for all. To help this book get you there, we have organized it into four sections. These sections are described here and portrayed in Figure 1.1.

Section 1: Setting the Stage. Chapters 1 and 2 make the case for the need to address the dropout problem and lay out the basics on how to get your dropout prevention planning process started.

Section 2: Understanding the Problem and Possible Solutions. Chapters 3 through 5 address the challenges associated with getting accurate dropout statistics and examine the reasons for, process of, and factors associated with dropping out.

Section 3: Putting the Pieces Together. Chapters 6 through 8 contain guidance on how to analyze existing programs and services, identify the needs of your district or school, and select a course of action designed to meet those needs.

Section 4: Implementation and Evaluation. Chapters 9 and 10 lead you through the process of how to implement your action plan and gather information to determine how effective it is in preventing students from dropping out of your school.

In addition, the book ends with three appendices that provide information useful while reading the book and information useful in the future.

Appendix A: Directory of Action Tools. List of all tools included in each chapter of the book.

Appendix B: Glossary. Terms used in the book, with brief definitions.

Appendix C: Related Links. List of organizations and Web sites with useful information on topics relevant to increasing school completion and decreasing dropout.

Chapter Format

The chapters in this book follow the same basic format. They start with a list of the main points covered in the chapter (Topics) followed by statements describing what you learn and do when you go through the chapter (In This Chapter, You Will . . .). A Myth or Truth? box, which contains true and false statements that you can identify at the beginning of a chapter, provides an advanced organizer for the chapter that is then revisited at the end of the chapter, where answers are provided as a check of your understanding.

An Implementation Scenario that is directly linked with chapter content is provided in chapters 2 through 10. The scenario illustrates an example of how the process of addressing dropout might unfold in a district or school setting. Each chapter includes a brief synopsis of the chapter's important points (Summary), followed by a set of Reflection Questions. These are designed to initiate discussion and broad thinking related to the chapter topic—to ensure that the knowledge that you have gained gets thought about several times and in different ways. After the Reflection Questions, each chapter has a list of books, articles, and other documents that are either referenced in the chapter or that provide further information (Further Reading).

Within the chapters you will find not only the information that gives you the knowledge that you need, but also the tools that you need to do something with the knowledge that you have gained. A section of planning and process activities is provided for those of you ready to begin gathering data, organizing, and problem solving issues that are directly related to addressing the problem of dropout in your own setting—this final section is called "Taking Action." The activities in this section are designed for individuals working on their own or in teams. Perhaps most important, each chapter provides a set of Action Tools, which includes forms, worksheets,

Table 1.1   Organization of Chapters

Topics	List of the main points covered in the chapter
In This Chapter You Will . . .	Statements describing what you will learn and do in the chapter
Myth or Truth?	Box with true and false statements that you can identify at the beginning of the chapter, and then can check with answers at the end of the chapter
	Body of Chapter Information on the chapter's topic, some of it highlighted in boxes and tables
Summary	Brief synopsis of the chapter's important points
Reflection Questions	Questions to initiate discussion and broad thinking related to the chapter topic
Further Reading	List of books, articles, and other documents either referenced in the chapter or that provide further information of interest
Taking Action	Section of action activities, designated for individuals or teams, with *Action Tools*, which are forms, worksheets, or other documents to guide you through the use of the tools; a *Guide to Action Tools* is provided as an overview to all tools in a chapter's *Taking Action* section

or other documents to guide you through various steps in the process. These and the Guide to Action Tools are a part of the Taking Action sections.

Because your progress through this book will be smoother if you really understand how it is laid out, we have included in Table 1.1 the general outline of each chapter. Understanding this before you start reading the chapters will serve you well, because at any point in time you will know where you are, where you have been, and where you are going!

Other Features of the Book

Evidence-Based Practices. This book is based on evidence-based practices and research. The reliance on research and scientific evidence permeates everything that we present, and was a primary consideration of whether general information, an example, or an action tool would be included.

User-Friendly Approach. Accompanying our belief in the need for evidence-based practices is our belief in the need for the information to be accessible by all. Thus, in this book, we have not provided academic references throughout the chapters. We refer to studies by name of investigator, as appropriate, and provide the references in the section on Further Reading at the end of each chapter. If there are questions about citations or sources of information, readers can contact us directly (see e-mail addresses in the Preface). We believe that this is preferable to bogging the text of this book down with traditional academic citations. We want this book to truly be a useful and practical guide to decreasing school dropout and increasing graduation for all.

Tools of Application. This book is not just a summary of research-based practices. We wanted to bridge research and practice and put it all together in one place—in a format accessible to all. We wanted readers to be able to go directly from knowledge acquisition to implementing that knowledge. The Action Tools at the end of each chapter provide this bridge.

SUMMARY

The purpose of this chapter was to get you on your way. We talked briefly about the importance of raising graduation rates, even though they are much higher today than they were 50 years ago. We highlighted not only the extensiveness of the dropout problem, but also the high costs to the individual and to society. With No Child Left Behind giving some emphasis to graduation rates, and many states requiring students to pass high-stakes exams to earn standard diplomas, we have our work cut out for us to promote graduation for all.

That is the purpose of this book, and in this chapter we have provided an overview of how we hope to get there. We give you tools to use and lots of pathways to follow to decrease school dropouts and pursue graduation for all. All chapters have knowledge, reflection, and doing actions for you.

Now, check your knowledge of the Myth or Truth? statements from the beginning of the chapter (see Box 1.2 for answers). How did you do? Were you able to explain why a statement was a myth or the truth?

Box 1.2   Myth or Truth? Answers

1. **Truth.** Those who drop out of school are more likely to be unemployed. *Explanation:* Research has confirmed that those who drop out of school are more likely to be unemployed. If they have jobs, those who dropped out of school are more likely not to use the skills that they do have. A high proportion of school dropouts end up in jails or prison. (See page 3.)

2. **Truth.** Dropouts tend to create significant costs to society. *Explanation:* Costs to society created by dropouts include lost tax revenues, increased welfare and unemployment costs, and increased prosecution and incarceration costs. (See pages 3–4.)

3. **Myth.** Most states met the goal of a 90% school completion rate in the year 2000. *Explanation:* Only 17 states met the goal of a 90% school completion rate in the year 2000. This goal was one that was set for states in 1990, so it was after 10 years that only 17 states met the goal. (See page 4.)

4. **Truth.** The percentage of students graduating from high school is an adequate yearly progress accountability indicator. *Explanation:* The No Child Left Behind Act requires that the percentage of students graduating from high school in four years with a standard diploma be an indicator in determining adequate yearly progress at the high school level. (See page 4.)

5. **Myth.** The No Child Left Behind Act requires graduation exams. *Explanation:* The No Child Left Behind Act does not require that states administer an exam to determine whether students earn a standard diploma. It does require that the percentage of students graduating from high school be one indicator in the determination of adequate yearly progress. (See page 5.)

FURTHER READING

Allen, L., Almeida, C., & Steinberg, A. (2004). *From the prison track to the college track: Pathways to postsecondary success for out-of-school youth.* Boston: Jobs for the Future.

Center on Education Policy. (2003). *State high school exit exams: Put to the test.* Washington, DC: Author.

Greene, J. (2001). *High school graduation rates in the United States* (rev. April 2002). Davie, FL: Manhattan Institute for Policy Research.

Greene, J. (2002). *Public school graduation rates in the United States* (Civic Report 31). Davie, FL: Manhattan Institute for Policy Research.

Joint Economic Committee. (1991, August). *Doing drugs and dropping out: A report prepared for the use of the subcommittee on economic growth, trade, and taxes of the Joint Economic Committee.* Washington, DC: U.S. Government Printing Office.

National Center for Education Statistics. (2002). *The condition of education 2002* (NCES 2002–025). Washington, DC: U.S. Department of Education, Office of Educational Research and Improvement.

National Commission on Excellence in Education. (1983). *A nation at risk: The imperative for educational reform.* Washington, DC: U.S. Government Printing Office.

U.S. Census Bureau. (2002). *The big payoff: Educational attainment and synthetic estimates of work-life earnings.* Retrieved July 29, 2004, from http://www.census.gov/prod/2002 pubs/p23–210/pdf

U.S. Census Bureau. (2003). *Educational attainment—People 25 years old and over, by total money earnings in 2002, work experience in age, race, Hispanic origin, and sex* (Table PINC-03). Retrieved July 29, 2004, from http://ferret.bls.census.gov/macro/032003/perinc/ new03_001.htm

2

Getting Started

TOPICS

- Considering Beliefs and Practices
- Organizing for Action
- Laying a Foundation

IN THIS CHAPTER, YOU WILL . . .

- Explore the meaning of a mission statement
- Learn about different ways to organize and connect with people in order to study the dropout problem
- Find out about how to share information with different audiences
- Think about the need for professional development
- Consider factors that impact readiness for addressing the dropout problem

If the need to solve your school's dropout problem is immediate, you may be tempted to turn to Chapter 8, select a program, and implement it. Or you might feel like calling up a neighboring school or district to see what it is doing, and then just do the same thing.

While those actions might get things moving initially, they probably will not serve you well in the long run. For one thing, you do not know whether the program being implemented down the road is appropriate for the needs of the students in your school. Nor can you be certain that what the other school is doing in the name of dropout prevention is based on effective practices. Most successful dropout prevention efforts are based on thoughtful planning and sound decision making—not quick fixes. You also need to consider how well the solution you are seeking is aligned with your district's mission, goals for student learning, and other efforts operating in your school. So, as tempting as it may be to just go find a dropout prevention program and implement it, simple and quick solutions carried out without

---

Box 2.1 Myth or Truth? Do You Know?

Read each statement following and decide whether it is a myth or the truth.

1. Most schools refer to their mission statements frequently and align their day-to-day practices with their mission statements.

2. There is only one way to organize a group of people to address the dropout problem.

3. Finding out if other groups might already be working on the dropout problem, or related challenges such as school safety, is a good preliminary step to take.

4. Devising a plan to share information with various audiences will help to prevent problems with miscommunication.

5. A school's previous experience with implementing new initiatives has no bearing on the success of future reform efforts.

---

regard to data-based student needs or evidence of effectiveness will probably not result in solving your dropout problem in the comprehensive way needed for success in the long term.

In this chapter, we address some "getting started" topics. First, we want you to revisit your mission statement and think about your dropout effort in light of it. Then, we provide some tips about ways to organize groups of people to work on dropout prevention efforts, and we offer ideas about how to get clear on who is doing what. We touch on professional development and ideas for how to go about sharing your plans with others. We conclude with some suggestions for determining your school's readiness to proceed down the path of assuring graduation for all students.

Before you begin, there are some statements in Box 2.1 for you to consider. You should be able to sort out which are the myths and which are the truths by the time you finish reading this chapter.

CONSIDERING BELIEFS AND PRACTICES

For change to occur, people may need to revisit what they think and do. You can start to do that by comparing what your school says it believes about students with its current practices.

Moving Your Mission Statement From Paper to Practice

All school districts have mission statements. They are usually posted on the walls, printed on the stationery, and inserted into everybody's handbooks. The few short sentences that make up a school's mission statement are often the result of a three-day retreat where everyone worked hard to come to agreement on the purpose of their school. But what happens to the mission statement after the retreat is over and the posters are printed?

Rick DuFour, in an article in the *Journal of Staff Development,* wrote about an informal survey he took of the ability of school districts to align "the noble sentiments of the mission statements and the reality of the day-to-day functioning of schools" (p. 68). DuFour wondered what would happen if schools were forced to write their mission statements as true portrayals of actual practice instead of lofty-sounding promises that are never fulfilled. If that were to happen, DuFour suggested that these words would be on some school walls instead: "Our mission is to help parents and the general public understand all the reasons that our students should not be expected to reach the standards of achievement that the state has established" (p. 69). According to DuFour, another school's mission statement might read:

> Our mission is to sort and select students into widely varying programs on the basis of their innate, fixed aptitude. We strive to present good lessons and to create classroom environments that encourage students to learn. We then rank them according to their willingness and/or ability to learn. Finally, we take credit for the achievement of high performing students and assign the blame for low performance. (p. 69)

Harsh as the words might sound, these mission statements may paint a more accurate picture of school life than the mission statements written in these schools' student handbooks. If you were to give an honest assessment of what your school really believes and put that into a statement, what would it say? Would it say that some students do not count and that if they left your classrooms you would not care? Or would it say that all students matter and that dropping out is just not an option in your school? Thinking, and maybe rethinking what you really believe about students completing school is an important first step in preventing school dropouts.

ORGANIZING FOR ACTION

The next step is to actually *do* something. Although you can do some of the work of solving the dropout problem on your own, other things may best be done by a group. If you want to get organized for action, there are several different approaches you can take depending on your circumstances.

Study Group

If your school or district is concerned about the dropout problem but is not quite ready to form an official group to work on it, you might start by forming a study group. This type of group comes together on a volunteer basis to study a topic of common interest. Membership is usually open to everyone, and schools that use this option routinely invite parents, paraprofessionals, and other school personnel to join the discussion. Tips for organizing a study group are in Table 2.1.

Action Team

If your school or district is ready to do some intensive work on the dropout problem, then an action team might be an option for you to consider. Unlike a study group, where the membership of the group is open to everyone, action team members are usually internal to the school or district, and they often represent areas affected by the issue being studied. An action team on dropout prevention might include teachers from general and special education and alternative schools,

Table 2.1 Study Group Guidelines

1. Keep the size of the group to no more than six.
2. Do not restrict the composition of the study group.
3. Establish and keep a regular schedule.
4. Establish group norms at the study group's first meeting.
5. Agree on an action plan for the study group.
6. Focus on curriculum and instruction.
7. List all learning resources, both material and human.
8. Complete a study group meeting log after each meeting.
9. Encourage members to keep a Personal Reflection Log.
10. Establish a pattern of rotating leadership.
11. Give all study group members equal status.
12. Plan for transitions.
13. Include training and other forms of staff development in the study group's agenda.
14. Evaluate the effectiveness of the study group.
15. Establish a variety of communication networks and systems.

SOURCE: Murphy, C. U. (1999). Use time for faculty study: Getting the whole faculty involved focuses a school. *Journal of Staff Development, 20*(2), 20–25. Adapted with permission of the National Staff Development Council, www.nsdc.org, 2004. All rights reserved.

along with guidance counselors, vocational counselors, principals, and attendance coordinators.

In addition to having knowledge of the dropout problem, there are other skills and abilities that an action team needs to function effectively. Finding members who have skills in areas like problem solving, data management, creative thinking, collaboration, conflict resolution, and written and oral communication will enhance the work of the team. An example of an action team is shown in Figure 2.1.

Community Advisory Committee

If you are at the point of needing broad input from the community on the dropout problem, you could form a community advisory committee. Unlike an action team, where the members are all internal to the school organization, a community advisory committee has members from groups that are "outside" of education. Types of community groups and agencies that could be represented on an advisory committee include:

- Chamber of Commerce
- Family and Community Services
- County Juvenile Department
- Park and Recreation
- Boys & Girls Clubs
- Mental Health Association
- Employment and Training Center
- Community College or Four-Year University
- Urban League

Figure 2.1   Example of Action Team

Name of Individual	Elementary Principal	Middle School Principal	High School Principal	Elementary Teacher	Middle School Teacher	High School Teacher	Alternative School Teacher	Guidance Counselor	Vocational Counselor	District Curriculum Coordinator	District Assessment Coordinator	Attendance Coordinator	Leadership	Written Communication	Oral Communication	Problem Solving	Collaboration	Data Analysis	Conflict Resolution	Creativity
1. Anderson, Amy			X										X	X		X	X		X	
2. Blanders, Brian								X							X	X			X	X
3. Cummings, Charles											X			X				X		X
4. Davidson, Daniel						X									X		X			
5. Elliot, Evelyn					X							X			X			X		
6. Franklund, Francine													X			X				X
7. Gregory, Georgina						X				X			X	X						
8. Henderson, Harry															X			X		

Table 2.2 Membership of Dropout Prevention Committees in Maine

Representative	Selected by
School board member	School board
School administrator	Superintendent
Teacher	Teacher's organization
School counselor	Teacher's organization
Parent	Organized parent group (if no organized parent group exists, by the school board)
School attendance coordinator	Superintendent
High school student	Dropout Committee members
Student who has dropped out	Dropout Committee members
Community resident	Dropout Committee members

SOURCE: *Title 20-A, Section 5103, dropout prevention committee.* (1989). Retrieved March 31, 2004, from http://janus.state.me.us/legis/statutes/20-A/title20-Asec5103.html. Adapted with permission from Maine State Department of Education, 23 State House Station, Augusta, ME 04333.

The state of Maine requires that each district form a dropout prevention committee with members from both the school and the community. Students and parents are also required members of dropout committees in that state. Table 2.2 lists the members and who selects each person.

LAYING A FOUNDATION

Besides thinking about your mission statement and organizing people to work on the challenge, there are some other steps you can take to ensure that your future dropout prevention efforts are built on a solid foundation. These preliminary planning activities include determining what other groups in your school or district might already be working on issues related to dropout prevention, sharing your plans with others, providing professional development, and considering your school's readiness to take on new challenges.

Connecting With Other Groups

It is possible, especially in a large district, not to know everything that is going on in other buildings in your district. Sometimes you may not even be aware of initiatives in your own school! So rather than reinvent the wheel, we recommend that you check to see whether there are other dropout prevention groups operating before beginning to work on the problem. If there are, connect with them to find out what they are doing and determine how their work connects with your efforts.

Besides gathering information about other dropout prevention efforts, you should also check to see if there are groups functioning with similar goals. For example, many schools have a school safety committee. This committee gathers information on issues like school climate, student use of alcohol and drugs, and school discipline, and then tries to correct the problems it identifies. Although the

Table 2.3   Groups Working on Issues Related to Dropout

- Citizen's Advisory Committee
- Graduation Task Force
- Health Services Committee
- Parent/Teacher Advisory Council on Discipline
- Community Service Learning Team
- School-to-Career Committee
- Comprehensive School Improvement Council
- English Language Learner Advisory Group
- Attendance Committee
- Educational Equity Task Force
- No Child Left Behind Committee

focus of a school safety committee is different from the work of a dropout prevention action team, there is enough overlap between the issues that both groups are studying to make taking the time to find out what they are doing a worthwhile activity. Other committees that could be operating in your school or district with similar goals that you might want to connect with are listed in Table 2.3.

The list in Table 2.3 is not exhaustive. We provide it to get you thinking about the need to connect with other groups before beginning your work. Finding out now who is doing what will save you time and serve you well in both the short and long term.

Sharing Information

Another step you can take now is to come up with a plan to keep people informed about what you are doing. Operating without some sort of communication plan in place and assuming that the necessary information will reach your intended audiences may result in people having a complete lack of information, too much information, or inconsistent or mixed messages.

These miscommunication scenarios can be avoided by thinking about the following questions:

- What are the key messages that need to be communicated?
- Who needs to hear these messages?
- What are the various types of communication devices that can be used to convey these messages?

You may decide that some of your early, key messages are to inform people of the dropout problem nationally, explain your local numbers, and announce that an action team has been appointed to address this issue. Next, you may determine that parents, the community, the staff, and the school board all need to hear those messages, but not through the same communication device. For the parents, you may decide to put an article in the parent newsletter. This same article can also be sent to the local paper and disseminated through an e-mail message to the staff. Providing a brief presentation to the board would complete this initial round of communication strategies.

Providing Professional Development

Another step you might take is to provide professional development for staff. Even without knowing exactly what you are going to do to resolve the dropout problem in your school, there are a number of training sessions that you can provide for staff that will help set the stage for the work that is to come. Possible professional development topics appropriate at this point in time are highlighted in Table 2.4.

Table 2.4   Professional Development Topics

- Adolescent mental health and the implications for learning
- Exploring effective conflict management strategies
- Improving school climate and increasing student motivation
- Partnering with parents to improve student learning
- How to gather, analyze, and use data
- Introduction to positive approaches to managing student behavior
- Cultural diversity and implications for the classroom
- Differentiated instructional strategies to improve academic achievement

Readiness for Change

Another way to put any future dropout prevention efforts on solid footing is to think about how ready your school or district is to pursue this work. One way to find out is to look at your school's track record with past initiatives and its current capacity in areas that will be important to solving your dropout problem.

Your school's history with planning and maintaining other educational initiatives is one predictor of what may be in store for you as you work on the dropout problem. If your school has not been successful in the past with planning and implementing new programs, it does not necessarily mean this effort will fail. It does mean that you will need to think carefully about previous stumbling blocks and figure out ways around them. Questions to help you sort out what might be potential trouble spots are listed in Table 2.5.

Another predictor of future success is the school's current capacity for carrying out activities critical to solving the dropout problem. A key aspect of this capacity is

Table 2.5   Questions for Assessing a School's Success With Past Initiatives

Does the school have a history of:

- Carrying out effective planning activities prior to implementing new programs and services?
- Maintaining new programs and services once they have been implemented?
- Sufficiently staffing and appropriately supervising new programs and services?
- Collaborating in meaningful ways with families and community agencies?
- Effectively addressing conflict or controversy?
- Encouraging shared leadership?
- Recognizing the need for and supporting professional development?

Table 2.6   Questions to Assess a School's Current Capacity for Starting a New Initiative

Does the school:

- Exhibit quality social relationships among students, teachers, administrators, parents, and community members?
- Have sufficient interest in solving the dropout problem?
- Work effectively with internal and external committees?
- Possess the resources necessary to support a dropout prevention planning process?
- Have a commitment to continuous improvement?
- Routinely collect various types of data and use the data to make decisions?
- Have resources to support professional development activities?

the quality of the social relationships that exist in your school. Research done by Anthony Bryk and Barbara Schneider found that high "relational trust" is central to successful school improvement efforts. Thinking about the strength of these relationships and other elements of educational capacity will help you in your planning process. Issues for you to think about are listed in Table 2.6.

If you identify past problems or current areas of organizational weakness, it will be important to try and address them before you start. Even if you cannot remove or reduce the barriers, just knowing that they exist will help you prepare for them as best you can. At least you will not be surprised when they arise. Keep them in mind, but keep moving forward.

Implementation Scenario: Getting Started (March/April/May)

As part of the state's continuous improvement plan, monies were designated to hold regional meetings with district-level superintendents focused on preventing dropout. Districts with a dropout rate of more than 10% were specifically targeted for attendance (based on year-end data for Grades 7–12). The use of graduation rates as measures of adequate yearly progress—designated in federal legislation—was highlighted. Superintendent LeGoode attended one of the regional meetings due to concerns about the low graduation rate in her district. In part, as a result of attending the regional meeting, Dr. LeGoode identified this issue as a district priority and convened a district-level meeting with administrative staff to address the problem. After a brief discussion, it became clear that a quick fix was not going to solve the problem. It was decided that a committee (action team) should be formed to work on developing a sound solution based on thoughtful planning and research. The committee would begin meeting in the fall, and committee members would be asked to make a long-term commitment to the project: the first year would focus on learning more about best practice approaches, developing a plan, and putting the plan into action. Care was taken to put a team together that included individuals in a variety of positions with relevant skills and abilities.

In addition, a community advisory group was formed that included many of the local community organizations focused on children and youth. The advisory group was formed to gather input from the broader community and facilitate support networks outside of the district education program. Initial steps that were decided upon early on included how to go about sharing information between groups and with the public. A communication plan was developed. In addition, time was spent considering how district-level professional development could be utilized to build a solid foundation of staff knowledge focused on keeping kids in school and providing skills necessary for successful graduation and post-school outcomes.

SUMMARY

The purpose of this chapter was to highlight some issues to consider and steps to take before proceeding with the challenge of solving the dropout problem in your school. We stressed the importance of really looking at your mission statement to see whether it accurately reflects what you do in practice. For readers wanting to work with others, we outlined a few ways to organize a group. We closed by providing you with a number of preliminary planning activities to help you lay the groundwork for the important work to come.

Now look at Box 2.2 for the answers to the Myth or Truth? statements presented at the beginning of this chapter. What are your explanations for why each statement was a myth or the truth? How did your explanations match up with those provided?

Box 2.2   Myth or Truth? Answers

1. **Myth.** Most schools refer to their mission statements frequently and align their day-to-day practices with their mission statements. *Explanation:* Although most schools have mission statements, their actual practices may not reflect the intent of their mission statements. (See page 13.)

2. **Myth.** There is only way to organize a group of people to address the dropout problem. *Explanation:* There is no one way to approach solving the dropout problem in a school. Some schools may organize informal study groups, while others might establish formal committees or teams to carry out the work that needs to be done. (See pages 13–16.)

3. **Truth.** Finding out if other groups might already be working on the dropout problem, or related challenges such as school safety, is a good preliminary step to take. *Explanation:* Many schools have a variety of committees addressing a wide range of topics, some of which are probably relevant to the dropout problem. Finding out what they are doing before starting a new initiative would prevent overlap of effort and provide valuable information. (See page 16.)

4. **Truth.** Devising a plan to share information with various audiences will help to prevent miscommunication. *Explanation:* A well-conceived communication plan will help ensure that key messages are delivered to the appropriate audiences through the most effective communication vehicles. (See page 17.)

5. **Myth.** Understanding a school's previous experience with implementing new initiatives has no bearing on the success of future reform efforts. *Explanation:* Knowing how well a school has dealt with past reform efforts can help to identify potential barriers to implementing new initiatives. (See pages 18–19.)

REFLECTION QUESTIONS

1. Why and how is the mission statement of a school relevant to the dropout problem?

2. In what ways can the school, the parents, the students, and the community work together to decrease the dropout rate?

3. Do you believe there are students in your school who will drop out no matter what? Why do you believe that?

FURTHER READING

Bryk, A. S., & Schneider, B. L. (2002). *Trust in schools: A core resource for improvement.* New York: Russell Sage Foundation.

DuFour, R. (2001). That's our mission? *Journal of Staff Development, 22*(1), 68–69.

Moving NSDC's staff development standards into practice: Innovation configurations. (2003). Oxford, OH: National Staff Development Council.

Murphy, C. U. (1999). Use time for faculty study: Getting the whole faculty involved focuses a school. *Journal of Staff Development, 20*(2), 20–25.

Murphy, C. U., & Lick, D. W. (2001). *Whole-faculty study groups: Creating student-based professional development* (2nd ed.). Thousand Oaks, CA: Corwin.

Scholtes, P. R., Joiner, B. L., & Streibel, B. J. (2003). *The team handbook* (3rd ed.). Madison, WI: Oriel.

Standards for staff development (rev. ed.). (2001). Oxford, OH: National Staff Development Council.

Title 20-A, Section 5103, dropout prevention committee. (1989). Retrieved March 31, 2004, from http://janus.state.me.us/legis/statutes/20-A/title20-Asec5103.html

TAKING ACTION

This section is for those of you who are ready to begin doing something to decrease the number of students dropping out of school. This requires taking action. If you are reading this book and working with a team of people, you will be acting as investigative reporters, trying to uncover information and clearly identifying what is happening in your setting. If you are reading this as an individual—perhaps a superintendent, school psychologist, or state-level specialist overseeing programming for students placed at risk—you can also work to locate existing data or collect information that will help to answer key questions and help you to lay the foundation for future initiatives, evaluate current efforts, or reflect on a course of action.

This chapter provided information about a number of issues that we think you should consider before actually working on the dropout problem. Possible readiness activities could include thinking critically about your school's mission and deciding if there is sufficient interest in and capacity for carrying out the work. Going through the process of deciding who will actually do the work and determining what other groups might be operating on similar issues could also serve as good places to begin.

Increasing staff skills through professional development opportunities appropriate to the dropout problem would almost certainly help to lay a solid foundation for the work to come.

Depending on your circumstances, there are a number of directions you can go from here. To determine what your next move should be, we recommend that you read through the statements in the left-hand column of the Guide to Action Tools, identify your most immediate needs, and then use the Action Tool listed in the right-hand column to help you meet that need. Be sure to check whether there are district or school policies or procedures that must be followed before proceeding with the activities you plan to carry out.

GUIDE TO ACTION TOOLS

What Do You Need to Know or Do?	Action Tool
Determine whether current school practices align with the mission statement	Action Tool 2.1: *Mission Statement Analysis Form*
Select individuals for an action team	Action Tool 2.2: *Action Team Selection Form*
Understand the work of other groups operating in the school or district with similar goals in order to coordinate your efforts with theirs	Action Tool 2.3: *Committee Mapping Form*
Identify possible organizational barriers and generate strategies for overcoming the barriers	Action Tool 2.4: *Readiness Questionnaire*
Communicate appropriate information to various individuals and stakeholder groups	Action Tool 2.5: *Communication Plan*

ACTION TOOL 2.1   MISSION STATEMENT ANALYSIS FORM

Objective: To determine whether current school practices align with the school's mission statement

Materials: Copy of your district or school mission statement; school handbooks (board, parent, teacher, and student)

Instructions:

1. Review the mission statement and write it on the Action Tool.

2. Review school handbooks to determine if the mission statement is included in them. Enter the results of your review on the Action Tool.

3. Generate a list of things you might see and hear in your school if your mission is being implemented as written, and enter that information on the Action Tool under the heading Possible Evidence.

4. Take a walk around your school to determine the presence or absence of the things you listed in Step 3. Look for signs, rules, posters, and so on. Listen to exchanges between adults and students. Also think about nonobservable practices (such as student grouping patterns or the level of student involvement in school matters) and what they convey about your beliefs. Record your thoughts on the Action Tool in the column under the heading Observed/Existing Evidence.

Follow-Up:

1. Summarize your findings, observations, and thoughts and enter that information at the bottom of the Action Tool.

2. Determine what actions, if any, you will take to align current school practices with your mission statement.

School/District _____

ACTION TOOL 2.1 MISSION STATEMENT ANALYSIS FORM

Mission Statement	Documents Containing Mission Statements	Possible Evidence	Observed/Existing Evidence
Summary Statement:			
Next Steps:			

25

ACTION TOOL 2.2   ACTION TEAM SELECTION FORM

Objective: To select individuals for the action team

Materials: List of all staff members

Instructions:

1. Generate a list of positions you want represented on the action team, such as high school principal, middle school teacher, alternative school teacher, guidance counselor, vocational counselor, or attendance coordinator. Place the selected positions across the top of the form in the section called Positions.

2. Brainstorm a list of skills and abilities that you think would enhance the work of the action team. You might consider skills and abilities in areas such as leadership, written communication, oral communication, problem solving, collaboration, data analysis, conflict resolution, or creativity. Place the selected skills and abilities across the top of the form in the section called Skills and Abilities.

3. Using the list of staff members, select individuals for the team and place their names on the form.

4. For each individual, place an X in the boxes on the form that represent their position in the school or district and the skills and abilities that person brings to the action team.

Adapted from *Comprehensive School Reform: Research-Based Strategies to Achieve High Standards*, copyright © 2000 WestEd. Used by permission of WestEd.

School/District _____

ACTION TOOL 2.2   ACTION TEAM SELECTION FORM

Name of Individual	Positions											Skills and Abilities											

ACTION TOOL 2.3   COMMITTEE MAPPING FORM

Objective: To understand the work of other groups operating in the school or district with similar goals in order to coordinate your efforts with theirs

Instructions:

1. Identify the names of the various groups. (See Table 2.3 for a list of possible groups to contact.)

2. Interview the chairperson of each group to determine the group's membership and purpose.

Follow-Up:

1. How does the work of the action team connect with each group?

2. How will the action team coordinate its work with the work of the other groups?

3. Who will take responsibility for ensuring that the connections are made?

28

School/District _____

ACTION TOOL 2.3   COMMITTEE MAPPING FORM

Name of Group	Members (Put an * by the name of the chairperson)	Purpose of the Group (Including goals and target audience)	Strategies for Connecting With the Action Team

ACTION TOOL 2.4   READINESS QUESTIONNAIRE

Objective: To identify possible organizational barriers and generate strategies for overcoming the barriers

Instructions:

1. Generate a list of questions about your school's past practices relative to implementing new initiatives (insert in Action Tool 2.4a) and its current capacity (insert in Action Tool 2.4b) for supporting work in the area of dropout prevention. (See Tables 2.5 and 2.6 for sample questions.)

2. Rate your school on each question and put an X in the appropriate column.

3. Provide sources of evidence or a rationale for each rating.

4. Identify possible barriers to initiating work on dropout prevention.

Follow-Up:

1. If there are barriers that might interfere with working on the dropout problem, how might you overcome them?

2. What assets did you identify? How can you use them to enhance your work?

3. Can all the information you have gathered be summarized in a few key statements?

4. What do you plan to do next?

School/District _____

ACTION TOOL 2.4a READINESS QUESTIONNAIRE

Past Practices

Question	Yes	For the Most Part	Some-what	No	Source of Evidence/ Rationale for Rating	Possible Barriers	Strategies for Overcoming Barriers

Summary Statement:

Next Steps:

ACTION TOOL 2.4b   READINESS QUESTIONNAIRE

Current Capacity

Question	Yes	For the Most Part	Some-what	No	Source of Evidence/ Rationale for Rating	Possible Barriers	Strategies for Overcoming Barriers

Summary Statement:

Next Steps:

ACTION TOOL 2.5   COMMUNICATION PLAN

Objective: To communicate appropriate information to various individuals and stakeholder groups

Instructions:

1. At the top of one sheet of paper, write the word *Audiences*. At the top of a second sheet of paper, write the word *Messages*. Write *Communication Tools* at the top of a third sheet.

2. Generate a list of individuals or groups who need to be informed, and put their names on the Audiences sheet of paper. This list might include school staff, students, the school board, families, the community, leaders of community organizations, and city officials.

3. Generate a list of key messages that you want to convey and put that information on the Messages sheet of paper. This might contain:
   • Information about national and local dropout rates
   • Commitment to working on the dropout problem
   • Names of action team members and how they were selected

4. Generate a list of different forms of conveying communication and put that information on the Communication Tools sheet of paper. This list might include memo, report, e-mail message, postings on the school's Web site, article in the newspaper, article in a school newsletter, a presentation, or a meeting.

5. Take the names of one individual or group from the Audiences list and put it in the Audience column on the Action Tool.

6. Keeping that individual or group in mind, select the message(s) from the Messages list that you think that individual or group needs to hear. (Remember that you can have more than one message for each person or group.) Enter that information in the Messages column on the Action Tool.

7. Select the method of communication from the list that is most appropriate for that individual or group and put it in the Communication Tool column on the Action Tool.

8. For each entry on the Action Tool (Communication Plan), consider who should prepare the information to be communicated and who should deliver the message. (Although most of the time the individual preparing the communication will also be the person who delivers the information, there are occasions when the preparation is done by one person and the delivery is done by another. For example, someone from the action team might write the memo to the staff about the dropout prevention work that the group is proposing to do, but the memo will be sent out under the superintendent's name.)

9. For each entry, determine when the communication task should be completed.

Follow-Up:

Once you have completed all the activities listed on your Communication Plan, consider the effectiveness of your strategies. What worked? What did not work? What will you do differently next time?

School/District _____

ACTION TOOL 2.5   COMMUNICATION PLAN

Audience	Messages	Communication Tool	Prepared by	Delivered by	Date Completed

3

Putting the Problem of Dropout in Context

Looking at the Numbers

TOPICS

- Variability in Statistics on Graduation and Dropout
- Dropout Rates for Student Subgroups
- Terminology
- Procedures for Calculating Rates

IN THIS CHAPTER, YOU WILL . . .

- Examine current graduation and dropout statistics and their variability
- Learn about ways to calculate graduation and dropout rates
- Explore your own numbers of graduates and dropouts

Just how big of a problem is the dropout problem? In Chapter 1, we mentioned the variability in graduation rates across the United States, and we also hinted at the complexities in calculating dropout rates. This suggests that there is confusion surrounding graduation rates—that suggestion is accurate. Of all the educational statistics that exist, dropout statistics are perhaps the most controversial and confusing. So, we need to spend a little time talking about them.

Box 3.1 Myth or Truth? Do You Know?

Read each statement following and decide whether it is a myth or the truth.

1. The U.S. graduation rate is consistently above 75%.

2. There is large variability among regions in graduation rates.

3. *Graduation* and *school completion* are terms that mean the same thing.

4. The best picture of dropouts as an outcome measure is provided by cohort rate formulas.

5. Cohort rates, status rates, and event rates all have uses in a successful dropout prevention program.

In this chapter, we address the problem of dropouts as a problem of numbers. Clearly this is just one aspect of the problem, but one with which you need to grapple if you are going to be able to determine whether you have a problem and whether you are having any success in dealing with it. You cannot know whether you have been effective in reducing your dropout rate unless you have defined how you count dropouts and have been doing it in a consistent manner for a while.

We address four topics in this chapter; our ultimate goal is that you end up with a definition of *dropout,* a way to count your dropouts, and tools that can help you not only in your counting, but also in knowing whether the number of students likely to enter the rolls of dropouts is going to increase. These are all essential for you to work successfully toward graduation for all and decreasing school dropouts.

First, we briefly summarize what we know about the numbers, especially dropout numbers and percentages, from national statistics. Second, we examine and compare the rates of dropout for students from different subgroups, including various ethnic and racial groups, and students with disabilities. Third, we look at the definitional issues surrounding the terms *graduation* and *dropout,* and explore their implications for how you look at them in your own district or school. Finally, we examine different ways to calculate dropout rates.

Before we get into these topics, test your knowledge by identifying the myths or truths in Box 3.1. Don't worry if they do not seem clear to you now. At the end of this chapter the answers and explanations are provided for your review.

VARIABILITY IN STATISTICS ON GRADUATION AND DROPOUT

We have already highlighted some of the national statistics that indicate that school dropouts are a problem in the United States today. National numbers consistently show that graduation rates are not what we would expect them to be. For example, the U.S. Department of Education has a Common Core of Data (CCD) that reveals for the year 2000–2001 the overall graduation rate was 68%. It is unfortunate that most of the national numbers that we have are fairly dated. This is because they take a long time to gather and summarize. (For schools and districts hoping to affect dropout rates, numbers have to be obtained and summarized much more quickly.)

We know that our nation has not been very successful in the past in meeting goals that were set for increasing graduation rates. There is variability among states, and there is variability among regions of the United States. Low and variable graduation rates, and dropout rates as well, are subject to another type of variability—one that is of critical concern here.

There is tremendous variability related to the way the terms *graduation* and *dropout* are defined. This variability can determine whether we think that our school or district has a problem that needs to be addressed, or whether we think that we have been successful in solving an existing problem. Changing a definition can have effects without even doing anything. For example, one state recently changed how it defined its graduation rate from "the percentage of students entering grade 12 who earn at the end of that year a high school diploma" to "the percentage of grade 9 students who 4 years later earn a high school diploma." With this change in definition, the graduation rate changed from 89% one year to 79% the next.

It is critical that you put the dropout problem in context and that you look at the numbers. Consider definitions currently used for *dropout* in the United States. The National Center for Education Statistics (NCES) uses the Common Core of Data (CCD). With these data, NCES generally uses a single-year definition of dropout, called an event rate (what percentage of students who were in school during this year dropped out) or a point-in-time definition, called a status rate (how many individuals ages 16–24 have not completed high school and are not enrolled).

The Office of Special Education Programs (OSEP) also collects exit data annually for students with disabilities. Unlike the NCES data, these data in the past have been based on students with disabilities who formally withdrew from school during the year based on all students with disabilities ages 14–22. Students with disabilities are one of the subgroups of particular interest for No Child Left Behind (NCLB) accountability calculations. For NCLB, the definitions of dropout and graduation for subgroups must be consistent with those used for other subgroups (more about this in the next section). The important point to remember is that the definition selected is going to have an impact on the information that is obtained from the numbers.

With the interest in graduation and dropouts, new ways of looking at the numbers are appearing. The Center for Social Organization of Schools at Johns Hopkins University has developed a measure called "promoting power" to serve as an indirect indicator of high dropout rates and low graduation rates. This measure compares the number of seniors in a high school to the number of freshmen four years earlier. The authors of the report *Locating the Dropout Crisis* recognize that while promoting power is not the same as graduation rate, it provides a pretty good indicator of the likelihood that the graduation rate will be high and the dropout rate will be low.

DROPOUT RATES FOR STUDENT SUBGROUPS

Two recent documents have highlighted the disparities in graduation rates and dropout rates among subgroups of students as well as across regions of the country and in states. In *Who Graduates? Who Doesn't?* the Urban Institute's Education Policy Center calculates a Cumulative Promotion Index (CPI) for each state and region for all students and for various breakdowns of student groups. This index is based on

Table 3.1 National and Regional CPI Graduation Rates, by Race and Ethnicity (2001)

	Census Region				
	Nation	*Northeast*	*South*	*Midwest*	*West*
All Students	68.0	71.0	62.4	74.5	68.2
Race/Ethnicity					
American Indian/AK Nat	51.1+	31.8+	58.1+	40.1+	50.7+
Asian/Pacific Islander	76.8	65.2+	81.9	75.5+	78.8
Hispanic	53.2	35.6+	55.4	53.1+	55.9
Black	50.2	43.8	52.3	46.5	54.2
White	74.9	78.7	68.9	78.7	75.0

NOTE: + Moderate Coverage: Rate covers between 50% and 75% of student population.

SOURCE: Common Core of Data, Local Educational Agency and School Surveys, National Center for Education Statistics. Reprinted with permission from C. B. Swanson (2003), *Who Graduates? Who Doesn't? A Statistical Portrait of Public High School Graduation, Class of 2001*, Washington, DC: Urban Institute, Education Policy Center, p. 20.

enrollment data. The report concludes, as is evident in Table 3.1, that there are wide national disparities among racial/ethnic groups, with a gap of about 25% between the highest and the lowest group, as well as variations that depend on the region. The report also concludes that some of the regional differences cancel each other out when aggregated to the national level.

Even though recognized as subgroups for No Child Left Behind purposes, most analyses of graduation rates and dropout rates in the past have not examined how students with disabilities and English Language Learners have fared in comparison to other students. If these subgroups are discussed, it tends to be as an explanation for the poor performance of a school. Data on the school completion of students receiving special education services are collected by the U.S. Department of Education, Office of Special Education Programs and summarized in the Annual Report to Congress on the Implementation of the Individuals with Disabilities Education Act.

Figure 3.1 shows the 2000 dropout exit data that were submitted by states to the U.S. Department of Education. One of the notable things about these data is that they cover students who are ages 14–21. Most graduation and dropout data represent cohorts of students—where the ninth grade cohort of students is four years later. The data in Figure 3.1 show a slight decrease in the percentage of students with disabilities dropping out across the years. The report indicates that this decrease was more evident in some disability categories:

> The biggest gains in the graduation rate were for students with multiple disabilities, speech/language impairments, emotional disturbance, autism, and deaf-blindness. Most of these are disability categories with the lowest graduation rates. It is unclear why some of the most significant disabilities showed increases in graduation rate; OSEP's longitudinal studies should help explain the change. Similarly, improvement in the dropout rate took place in almost every disability category, most notably among students with speech/language impairments, specific learning disabilities, orthopedic impairments, hearing impairments, and emotional disturbance. (U.S. Department of Education, p. IV-8)

Figure 3.1 Dropout Exit Data From Annual Report to Congress (1999–2000)

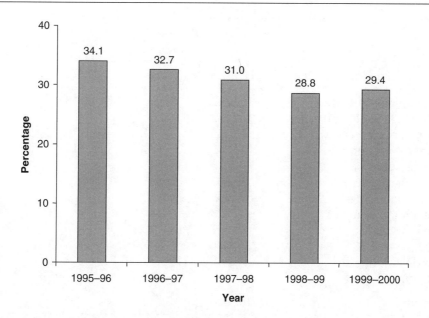

NOTE: Dropout rates were calculated by dividing the number of students 14 and older who dropped out by the number of students 14 and older who graduated with a diploma, received a certificate, reached the maximum age for services, died, or dropped out.

SOURCE: U.S. Department of Education, Office of Special Education Programs, Data Analysis System. Reprinted from Figure IV-2, Percentage of Students Age 14 and Older Dropping Out, 1995–96 to 1999–2000, 24th Annual Report to Congress, 2002. Retrieved from http://www.ed.gov/about/reports/annual/osep/2002/section-iv.doc

What is extraordinary—and hidden in Figure 3.1—are the actual dropout percentages for some of the disability categories. Graduation rates and dropout rates for each of the 13 disability categories for 1999–2000, the most recent data available in 2004, when this book was written, are displayed in Table 3.2. For example, the percentage of students with emotional/behavioral disabilities dropping out of school was about 50%. Nearly one-fourth of students with learning disabilities dropped out of school. Again, the critical point here is that it is important to pay attention to subgroups. This is going to affect how numbers are collected and how programs are planned.

There are a couple of additional points that are important. For years, OSEP has had a category of "Moved, Not Known to Continue," which was a separate count of students who could not be located—no one knew whether they had moved to another school or another state, or whether they had dropped out of school. In summaries such as that in Table 3.2, these students are not included—they simply disappear from all calculations. Yet, the number of these students is not trivial. In fall 2004, the "Moved, Not Known to Continue" group was going to be added to the "Dropped Out" group. According to reporter Arundel, recalculations of data from 2000–2001 showed that the effect of the change was to decrease the graduation rate from 61% to 51%, and to increase the dropout rate from 26% to 38% overall.

Losing Our Future: How Minority Youth Are Being Left Behind by the Graduation Rate Crisis is another document that highlights the disparities in graduation rates among student subgroups, focusing again primarily on the racial/ethnic subgroups. It argues for the need to pay attention to subgroup dropout rates, not just overall rates. It reiterates the finding of a significant dropout crisis for certain

Table 3.2   Special Education Categories Graduation and Dropout Rates
(Students Age 14 and Older, 1999–2000)

Disability Category	Graduated With a Standard Diploma		Dropped Out	
	Number	Percentage	Number	Percentage
Specific learning disabilities	109,012	62.1	48,490	27.6
Speech or language impairments	4,802	66.1	1,787	24.6
Mental retardation	16,425	39.5	10,812	26.0
Emotional disturbance	14,842	40.1	19,032	51.4
Multiple disabilities	2,676	48.0	896	16.1
Hearing impairments	2,862	68.4	620	14.8
Orthopedic impairments	2,055	62.5	506	15.4
Other health impairments	7,325	67.7	2,423	22.4
Visual impairments	1,157	73.4	187	11.9
Autism	578	47.3	135	11.1
Deaf-blindness	47	48.5	10	10.3
Traumatic brain injury	799	65.3	221	18.1
All disabilities	162,580	56.2	85,119	29.4

NOTE: The percentages in this table were calculated by dividing the number of students age 14 and older who graduated with a standard diploma by the number of students age 14 and older who are known to have left special education (that is, graduated with a standard diploma, received a certificate of completion, reached the maximum age for services, died, or dropped out). Washington State data based on previous year's data.

SOURCE: U.S. Department of Education, Office of Special Education Programs, Data Analysis System (DANS). Reprinted from Table IV-1, Number and Percentage of Students Age 14 and Older With Disabilities Graduating With a Standard Diploma or Dropping Out, 1999–2000, 24th Annual Report to Congress, 2002. Retrieved from http://www.ed.gov/about/reports/annual/osep/2002/section-iv.doc

groups of students—primarily Black, Native American, and Hispanic males, whose graduation rates are only around 45%. Further, it states that "dropout data mislead the public into thinking that most students are earning diplomas" (p. 4). What is the document's explanation for this statement? Here is another statement from the document: "Incredibly, some states report a 5% dropout rate for African Americans, when, in reality, only half of their young adult African Americans are graduating with diplomas." It is important to understand what is behind statements like these— and to know how the components influence your considerations for attacking the dropout problem and the challenge of increasing graduation for all in your school.

TERMINOLOGY

The academic literature discusses "school completion" as a concept that is broader than graduation. It includes the idea that a student successfully finishes school without regard, necessarily, to doing so within a specific time period nor necessarily to doing so by receiving a specific piece of paper to indicate a certain type of accomplishment.

What does this conjure up in your head? For sure, it includes students who receive a *standard diploma* in four years after Grade 9. But, it also includes students who take five years to earn that standard diploma. And, in states that have a graduation exam that students have to pass, it includes students who do not pass that exam but who complete all coursework and receive a basic *diploma* or a *certificate of completion*. It also includes students who receive a *special education diploma* in states and districts that award those. Furthermore, it might include students whose high schools acknowledge *General Education Development (GED) diplomas* as an avenue to school completion.

This broad all-encompassing view of school completion is not necessarily one that is in line with current views of graduation, which are more often time-delineated and focused on the receipt of certain types of credentials. Thus, the term *graduation* has come to mean something more specific than the term *school completion*.

Graduation

Graduation conjures up images of students moving across the stage to be awarded a diploma and have the tassel on their mortarboard moved from one side to the other. It is a vision of meeting standards that indicates that the student has a certain level of knowledge and skills. Often, the standard diploma or "higher" diplomas (such as *honors diplomas* or special endorsements) are the only diplomas that count as indicators of graduation. Certificates of attendance, special education diplomas, and more recently (such as in the No Child Left Behind Act), taking too long to earn a standard diploma—say five years instead of four—do not earn the school accountability points (unless a variation from the standard definition has been approved as part of the school accountability plan). In an analysis of NCLB accountability plans, Erpenbach, Forte-Fast, and Potts found that several states did request a variation in their definition of *graduation rate*, but that these variations were limited and did not go beyond the standard diploma. The primary exception was to allow an extra year to obtain a standard diploma when this was consistent with an educational philosophy already evident, or to allow the Individualized Educational Program (IEP) teams for students with disabilities to determine the number of years to obtain a standard diploma. GEDs or other types of exit documents were not allowed to be included in the graduation rate calculations for NCLB accountability.

Dropout

As we have already noted, dropout numbers are subject to wide definitional confusion. As implemented in schools today, there is wide variation in the grades and age levels in which students can be classified as dropouts. In some locations, students are not counted as dropouts if they are in the ninth grade; in other places, they are. Another source of variation is the amount of time that students can miss school with unexcused absences before they are considered to be dropouts. In one place it may be 15 days, and in another it may be 45 days. The amount of time included in the accounting period during which dropout is calculated is another factor that affects the dropout rate—looking across a single year is likely to produce much lower numbers than looking across several years. All of these factors are complexities that contribute to the difficulty of determining whether an individual student really is a dropout. A further illustration of the complexities and their implications both for calculating dropout numbers and for identifying students who are, or are about to become, dropouts is provided in Box 3.2.

Finally, who is included in the student population to begin with is a big part of what the dropout numbers end up looking like. Some programs have decided to exclude whole populations, such as their special education students or students who

---

Box 3.2   Example of Complexities of Defining and Counting Dropouts

Even when a definition of *dropout* sounds simple, it has hidden complexities that need to be resolved to be able to determine how to keep track of whether students are dropouts. A simple component of many definitions of dropout is that the student is absent without an excuse *x* number of days. Here are some of the complexities of that simple component, reflected in questions that would be raised as a school began to consider how to track that component:

- What is the specific definition of *unexcused*? Is the student considered to have an unexcused absence for the day if the student showed up for first hour class and was counted as present, but then did not make it to the rest of his or her classes (assuming attendance is taken in other classes)? Does it matter what the reason is for not making it to the rest of the classes (for example, went to nurse's office because sick, went to office for behavioral referral, skipped classes)?
- Is there a time frame for the absent days? If the student does not have the *x* number of unexcused absent days within the same semester or quarter, does this count? Is the time frame the length of a period of schooling or the entire school year?
- How complicated is the attendance policy? If the student is present at the beginning and end of the day, is that considered in attendance that day? Or, does the student have to be counted as present during a roll call at the beginning of each class period? Or, does the student have to be in each class for a certain period of time to be considered present?

These are only the beginning of the complexities that can be raised. But, it is well worth the time taken to think about all the complexities, and about how complex your school wants to get in the operationalization of its definitions. These decisions have implications for the mechanisms that are needed to track students to determine whether they are dropouts.

---

have decided to pursue a GED. Districts have many programs in which they have students—alternative programs or charter schools, for example—where decisions are made that affect the dropout count. These kinds of decisions often are hidden. They should not be. This is just one aspect of knowing your numbers. As the Education Trust indicated in *Telling the Truth*, a great exposé on how true numbers can be hidden, the long-term success of any improvement strategy really is having good information. Knowing your numbers and determining your own specific procedures for calculating rates is one key to having good information.

PROCEDURES FOR CALCULATING RATES

Traditional information on calculating dropout statistics starts with making distinctions among three types of formulas that are used to calculate dropout rates. It is important to understand these types of formulas. It is also important to determine what other kinds of information you need to gather.

Dropout Formulas

Three types of formulas are used to calculate dropout rates: cohort, status, and event. *Cohort rate* formulas, which measure what happens to a single group of students over a period of time, are generally believed to give the best picture of dropouts. It is the formula that typically yields the highest numbers because it uses a longitudinal approach. The longer the time period for which students are followed, the more difficult it is to keep track of students, but also, the more likely it is that some students will drop out. A cohort rate formula is what the No Child Left Behind Act is requiring states to use for the Adequate Yearly Progress (AYP) accountability measure—states must submit the percentage of ninth grade students who graduate with a standard diploma four years after their ninth grade year, unless they have received approval for an exception.

Status rate formulas give a snapshot picture of a group's status at a given point in time. The National Center for Education Statistics (NCES) reports status dropout rates when it cites information on the percentages of youth ages 16–24 who have not completed high school and are not enrolled in a high school program. There are ways in which status rates might be useful for a district or school to gain information that will help it in addressing its dropout problem—such as identifying the numbers of students who are of sophomore age, for example, who have not accrued enough credits to be on track to graduate in another two years. But, the usefulness of the status rate for specifically measuring dropouts is probably not relevant for schools and districts simply because it does not tell us enough.

The formula that gives the smallest rate of dropouts is the *event rate* formula. This statistic measures the number of students who drop out of school in a single school year—out of the students who started the school year. Of course, it misses the many students who decide never to set foot in the school again after the summer is over. This rate is referred to as an *annual rate* or an *incidence rate*. While it is not a good measure for a district or a school to adopt as an outcome measure, it has some usefulness in measuring program effectiveness. If you have developed a program designed to keep kids in school, you may want to measure how many of the students who are in that program drop out of school. This specific use of this statistic might make sense.

Table 3.3 is a summary of the dropout statistics and how they might be used within a district or school. It is important to remember that all statistics have advantages and disadvantages. It is the assumptions that you make and the numbers that you put in that determine whether the information you obtain will be useful to you. But, it is always more useful to have information to look at than to have none.

Implementation Scenario: Putting the Problem of Dropout in Context: Looking at the Numbers (September/October)

The district-level committee began meeting regularly once every two weeks. As well as examining the issue at a district level, three schools—one elementary (K–6), one middle school (7–8), and one high school (9–12)—were invited to work intensively with the district committee to address dropout prevention with their staff and students. Representatives from the schools who also attended the district-level meetings included the principal, counselor/school psychologist, and a regular education teacher. Members of each of the three school-level committees were selected with attention to utilizing the skills and abilities of a variety of stakeholders, including special and regular education teachers, parents, support staff, paraprofessionals, and others.

Table 3.3 Dropout Statistics and Ways That They Might Be Used

Dropout Statistic	What It Is	Ways to Use
Cohort Rate	Rate at which students in a group (e.g., 9th graders) drop out over a certain period of time (e.g., 4 yrs)	Outcome Measure • Overall • Student subgroups
Status Rate	Rate at which students have certain characteristics at a certain point in time *Examples:* Percentage of students who are of sophomore age who have the number of credits to be on track to graduate in another two years Pregnant students not returning to school	Warning Measure • Identify at-risk groups needing interventions
Event Rate	Rate at which students who enter a program drop out within a single year or term	Program Evaluation • Dropout prevention program • Alternative education program

After the school and district groups were formed, one of the first formal activities was to establish or renew a commitment to keeping all kids in school and helping them to complete school—even those students with challenging home situations, behavior or academic problems. Although somewhat heated, participants thought this discussion and the analysis of existing mission statements was especially useful for getting everyone on the same page.

Next, the district- and school-level committees needed to determine the magnitude of the dropout problem. First, the committee members looked for existing information that was already being collected. For example, the state tracked and compiled the number of students who graduated, dropped out, or continued schooling in four years as part of a completion study for ninth grade cohorts. Upon closer examination of the data, the committee realized the numbers excluded students whose whereabouts were unknown. In addition, students who completed GEDs or graduated in more than four years were not followed or counted. This raised questions about how dropout and graduation were defined. State, district, and school definitions were gathered and compared. Committee members were surprised to find that the system used to track students was cumbersome and did not provide the whole picture. As a result, the district committee developed recommendations for how to define dropout and graduation, and a way of obtaining the most accurate and meaningful information in a timely manner.

SUMMARY

The purpose of this chapter was to begin to look at the numbers of dropout and to put some context around them. We briefly reviewed some of the national statistics, highlighting the variability across regions, states, and across subgroups of students.

The variability is important because it has implications for how you look at numbers within your district or school. If you look at only one number—such as a dropout rate for the school—some important information is probably being lost. And, the information that is lost probably has important implications for your programs for reducing dropouts and increasing graduation rates.

In this chapter we also began to explore ways in which dropout and graduation could be defined. These form the basis for thinking about and beginning to look at your own numbers. The numbers are very important. They help you pinpoint where your problems lie. And, they help you determine whether you are being successful. Scrimping on the numbers will do you in—in the end!

Now check your knowledge about the Myth or Truth? statements from the beginning of the chapter (see Box 3.3 for answers). How did you do? Were you able to explain why a statement was a myth or the truth?

Box 3.3   Myth or Truth? Answers

---

1. **Myth.** The U.S. graduation rate is consistently above 75%. *Explanation:* The overall graduation rate was 68% in 2000–2001. The U.S. graduation rates are lower than many people think they are. (See page 36.)

2. **Truth.** There is large variability among regions in graduation rates. *Explanation:* Variability in graduation rates among regions is great, ranging from 62% to 75% in 2000–2001. (See page 38.)

3. **Myth.** *Graduation* and *school completion* are terms that mean the same thing. *Explanation: School completion* is usually defined as a broader term than *graduation*. It includes students who finish school in a variety of ways—for example, with a certificate of attendance—that might not be counted in a graduation definition. (See pages 40–41.)

4. **Truth.** The best picture of dropouts as an outcome measure is provided by cohort rate formulas. *Explanation:* Cohort rate formulas measure what happens to a single group of students over a period of time. (See pages 42–43.)

5. **Truth.** Cohort rates, status rates, and event rates all have uses in a successful dropout prevention program. *Explanation:* Cohort rates can be used as outcome measures; status rates can be used as warning measures; event rates can be used as program evaluation measures. (See page 43.)

REFLECTION QUESTIONS

1. What does it mean to complete school in your state and your district? Are they the same? What is your definition of *graduation*?

2. When does a student get counted as a "school dropout"? Does your school have policies in place that establish the amount of time that a student has to miss school with unexcused absences before the student is considered a dropout?

3. Who is responsible for keeping track of students and noting whether they are dropouts? What mechanisms are in place to keep track of these students?

FURTHER READING

Arundel, K. (2004, July 29). ED to seek recalculation of special ed graduation rates. *Education Daily, 37*(143), 1, 3.

Balfanz, R., & Legters, N. (2004). *Locating the dropout crisis: Which high schools produce the nation's dropouts? Where are they located? Who attends them?* Baltimore, MD: Johns Hopkins University, Center for Social Organization of Schools.

Education Trust. (2003). *Telling the whole truth (or not) about high school graduation.* Washington, DC: Author.

Erpenbach, W. J., Forte-Fast, E., & Potts, A. (2003). *Statewide educational accountability under NCLB: Central issues arising from an examination of state accountability workbooks and U.S. Department of Education reviews under the No Child Left Behind Act of 2001.* Washington, DC: Council of Chief State School Officers, State Collaborative on Assessment and Student Standards—Accountability Systems and Reporting.

Lehr, C. A., Johnson, D. R., Bremer, C. D., Cosio, A., & Thompson, M. (2004). *Essential tools: Increasing rates of school completion: Moving from policy and research to practice.* Minneapolis: University of Minnesota, National Center on Secondary Education and Transition.

Orfield, G., Losen, D., Wald, J., & Swanson, C. B. (2004). *Losing our future: How minority youth are being left behind by the graduation rate crisis.* Cambridge, MA: The Civil Rights Project at Harvard University.

Swanson, C. B. (2003). *Who graduates? Who doesn't? A statistical portrait of public high school graduation, class of 2001.* Washington, DC: Urban Institute, Education Policy Center.

U.S. Department of Education. (2002). *Twenty-fourth annual report to Congress on the implementation of the Individuals with Disabilities Education Act.* Washington, DC: Author.

TAKING ACTION

A discussion about dropout and graduation numbers just begs for you to go to the next step and begin to look at your own numbers. This section is designed to help you do that—to systematically begin to think about (1) the types of variables that need to be included in your numbers, (2) the procedures that you have in place to get at the numbers, and (3) the mechanisms that you need to set up to get at the numbers. As you address these, you will find that you are addressing your core beliefs and assumptions about who must count and be counted in your educational system.

The first step that you need to take is to reach agreement on how you are going to define your terms for the purposes of keeping track of numbers. Another step is to address how to keep track of students—to determine when individuals are staying in school or are slipping away. Finally, you will want to determine what the numbers mean by actually working with some of your own numbers.

Whether you are working on your own, or you are working with a group, this is a good time to determine what your next move should be before you go on to Chapter 4. Read through the questions on the left side of the Guide to Action Tools, to identify your most immediate need or needs, and then use the Action Tool that is listed in the right-hand column that will help you meet your identified need or needs. Remember, the Action Tools are samples of forms that may help you as an individual or a group within your school or district. The tools can be reproduced. But, they can also be used as a springboard for something that may better meet your needs. Be sure to check whether there are district or school policies or procedures that must be followed before proceeding with the activities you plan to carry out.

GUIDE TO ACTION TOOLS

What Do You Need to Know or Do?	Action Tool
Identify the current student makeup of the school	Action Tool 3.1: *Student Demographic Information Sheet*
Identify the diploma options available to students in your district and which students are receiving each option	Action Tool 3.2: *District/School Diploma Options Form*
Clarify the definitions used in your district and state for *school completion, graduation,* and *dropout*	Action Tool 3.3: *Definition Grid*
Determine considerations for tracking students related to dropout definition	Action Tool 3.4: *Student Tracking Tool*
Check numbers using different dropout definitions	Action Tool 3.5: *Dropout Calculation Form*

ACTION TOOL 3.1   STUDENT DEMOGRAPHIC INFORMATION SHEET

Objective: To gather information on student demographics in your school so that you have a "big picture" of all students

Materials: District data base or school rosters

Instructions:

1. Enter on the Action Tool the grades for which you are interested in gathering data.

2. Inquire about the availability of data from a central source. Determine whether all or some of the breakdowns are available to you.

3. After obtaining available data and filling in the Action Tool (or one that you have adjusted to meet your needs), use your own school rosters to fill in missing data (data not available from a district database).

4. If there is time available, check your own counts against counts provided by the district database.

Follow-Up:

1. Look at the distribution as a whole of the student population in your school. Compare and contrast numbers among subgroups. Are there unique or unexpected distributions? Enter observations of anything unusual into the Summary Statement box.

2. If you are in a group, discuss the pattern of distributions. Share with community members to determine whether there is anything unexpected from the community's perspective.

School/District _____

ACTION TOOL 3.1   STUDENT DEMOGRAPHIC INFORMATION SHEET

	Grades			
Total Population				
Socioeconomic Status (Average)				
English Language Learners (Percentage and primary non-English language group)				
Disability (Percentage)				
Race/Ethnicity (Percentage and by subgroup)				
Male:Female Ratio				
Retention Rate (Average percentage)				
Others				
Summary Statement:				

ACTION TOOL 3.2   DISTRICT/SCHOOL DIPLOMA OPTIONS FORM

Objective: To determine the number of diploma options available in your district and the percentage of students receiving each option

Materials: District or state graduation policy

Instructions:

1. List the different exit documents that students can receive in your district (for example, standard diploma in four years, certificate of attendance, special education diploma). Extend this list by adding different ways in which the documents can be earned (see examples given in Action Tool 3.2).

2. For each option, indicate the percentage of each group within each category earning each type of exit document.

Follow-Up:

1. Within each category at the top of the Action Tool, look at the distribution across the diploma options. Does there seem to be a disproportionate percentage of students not receiving a standard diploma in four years? Record your observations in the Summary Statement.

2. Look at patterns across all groups. Are patterns the same? If so, is the pattern what it should be? If not, for which groups is the pattern more like what you want, and for which groups is it less like what you want?

School/District _____

ACTION TOOL 3.2   DISTRICT/SCHOOL DIPLOMA OPTIONS FORM

Options	Gender		English Language Learner?		Race/Ethnicity (e.g., Asian, Black)	Disability (e.g, LD, EBD)	Low SES?	
	Male	Female	Yes	No			Yes	No
Standard diploma in four years from Grade 9								
Standard diploma in five or more years from Grade 9								
Certificate of completion/attendance								
Special education diploma								
GED diploma								
Honors/Advanced diploma								
Others								
Summary Statement:								

ACTION TOOL 3.3   DEFINITION GRID

Objective: To clarify the definitions used in your district and state for *school completion, graduation,* and *dropout*

Materials: District graduation policies and other documents that might contain definitions of school completion, graduation, and dropout; similar documents from the state and another district, if possible

Instructions:

1. Find definitions within district and state graduation policies for the terms *school completion, graduation* or *graduate,* and *dropout,* and enter these on the Action Tool.

2. Separate the state and district definitions if you have separate state and district policies.

Follow-Up:

1. Discuss the following points:
   - Could you find definitions in the policies? For all terms?
   - Are terms defined in different ways in different documents?
   - How do definitions in your district compare to definitions in other districts?
   - How do definitions in your district compare to state definitions?

2. Record observations in the Summary Statement box.

School/District _____

ACTION TOOL 3.3   DEFINITION GRID

Term to Define	District Definitions	Comparison Definition: State	Comparison Definition: Another District
School Completion			
Graduation or Graduate			
Dropout			
Summary Statement:			

ACTION TOOL 3.4   STUDENT TRACKING TOOL

Objective: To identify critical elements of the district's definition of *dropout* and how each is tracked for individual students

Materials: District dropout definition, policies, and guidelines

Instructions:

1. Read through all information to glean all the details of what the elements of the dropout definition really are (see examples in Action Tool 3.4). Place your own elements in a tool that you develop for your own use.

2. Develop a narrative that describes the mechanics of how the individual student is tracked to the point that the school or district is able to identify that student as a school dropout.

Follow-Up:

1. Identify the points, if any, at which it is possible for a student to slip between the cracks, and not be tracked as a dropout.

2. Are there natural points where it might be possible to involve an individual to ensure that the data for tracking individual students would be more accurate than they are now?

School/District _____

ACTION TOOL 3.4   STUDENT TRACKING TOOL

District Definition of _School Dropout:_

Critical Elements in Definition That Must Be Tracked	Mechanism in Place in School for Tracking for Individual Students	Complexities in Tracking Element
Example: 14 consecutive days unexcused absences	_Example: Aide enters excused absences into computer program on day of absence, so unexcused absences are known on same day_	_Example: If "day" is other than full day, a more complicated way of accounting for absences is needed_

ACTION TOOL 3.5   DROPOUT CALCULATION FORM

Objective: To calculate dropout rates using different types of dropout definitions

Materials: Numbers of students in each grade, Grades 9–12, for the past four years

Instructions:

1. List the data that you have from your district (numbers of students in each grade in each of the past four years).

2. Review the three types of dropout definition approaches (cohort, status, event).

3. Apply the definitions to your data. Using the data on numbers of students from your district, make rough calculations of dropout for your district for the year before this one (if those data are available to you).

Follow-Up:

1. Consider the numbers that you obtained. Did the cohort rate definition produce the highest number of dropouts? Why would this approach be considered an outcome measure?

2. Discuss the status rate numbers that you obtained. This dropout statistic has been considered to be a warning measure. If it is a warning, what does this say about your district's data? Does this seem realistic?

3. Discuss the event rate numbers that you obtained. This dropout statistic is considered useful for program evaluation. Why might this be the case?

4. Write overall observations from the Action Tool (Dropout Calculation Form) in the Summary Statement box.

School/District _____

ACTION TOOL 3.5   DROPOUT CALCULATION FORM

Definition	Your Numbers
Cohort Rate: Rate at which students in a group (such as ninth graders) drop out over a certain period of time (for example, four years)	
Status Rate: Rate at which students have certain characteristics at a certain point in time (for example, percentage of sophomore-age students who have number of credits needed to graduate in another two years)	
Event Rate: Rate at which students who enter a program drop out within a single year or term	
Summary Statement:	

4

Understanding Why

Looking at the Reasons, the Process, and the Approach

TOPICS

- Why Students Drop Out of School
- Why Students Stay in School
- Dropout: A Process of Disengagement
- A Focus on Completing School

IN THIS CHAPTER, YOU WILL . . .

- Learn about reasons why students drop out of school
- Learn about reasons why students stay in school
- Examine dropout as a process of disengagement that begins early
- Find out why focusing on school completion can strengthen intervention efforts
- Examine what is happening in your setting

Why do some students drop out of school, and why do others remain in school until they have received a diploma? When do students start to lose interest in completing school, and what can we do to keep students on track to graduate? These are some of the questions that we address in this chapter. Listening to the reasons students give for leaving and for staying in school provides you with a better understanding of

---

Box 4.1   Myth or Truth? Do You Know?

Read each statement following and decide whether it is a myth or the truth.

1. Competing forces outside of school such as getting a job or having a child to care for are the most frequently cited reasons for dropping out of school.

2. Students are more likely to stay in school when they participate in school and feel a strong connection or identification with their school.

3. The decision to drop out of school often occurs suddenly, with little warning.

4. Most students who drop out of school never return to school and do not obtain a diploma or equivalent degree.

5. Strategies that engage children and youth in school and learning are the key to keeping kids in school and raising graduation rates.

---

how to deal with dropouts. Information describing the process of dropout also can serve as a strong foundation for effective ways of increasing the number of students who complete school successfully. This chapter emphasizes the importance of a conceptual shift in thinking—toward building connections that facilitate school completion, rather than decreasing the rate of dropout.

Before going any further, test your knowledge by identifying the myths or truths for this chapter in Box 4.1. The answers and explanations for them are provided at the end of the chapter.

WHY STUDENTS DROP OUT OF SCHOOL

To understand a problem, it is often helpful to talk with individuals who have experienced the situation firsthand. To better understand dropout, researchers have asked students why they drop out of school. The answers from students have shown that the reasons for dropout are many and varied. Some students drop out because they do not like school in general. Others drop out because of competing responsibilities, which may include working at a job for pay or raising and caring for a child during high school. There are often multiple reasons for a student's ultimate decision to drop out.

Pushing and Pulling Students Out of School

Explanations for dropping out of school have been organized into two broad categories—called *push and pull effects*. Some of these are listed in Table 4.1. When nearly 1,000 students were asked to select from a list of 21 statements the reasons why they left school early, many selected responses indicating school factors that tend to *push* students out of school. These reasons included not liking school, not keeping up with school work, and not getting along with teachers. Educational researchers Will Jordan, James McPartland, and Julia Lara described push effects as being:

Table 4.1   Reasons Students Drop Out of School

Why Students Drop Out of School	
Push Effects	*Pull Effects*
Did not like school	Had to get a job
Could not get along with teachers	Wanted to have a family
Could not get along with students	Was pregnant
Suspended too often	Had to support family
Did not feel safe at school	Wanted to travel
Expelled from school	Friends dropped out
Did not belong	Got married, or planned to get married
Could not keep up with school work	Had to care for family member
Failing school	

located within the school itself. They cause adolescents to feel unwelcome, resist, or altogether reject schooling. The rejection of school by potential dropouts can manifest in disruptive behavior, chronic absenteeism, and/or a complete cessation of academic effort. However, in punishing this kind of behavior by suspending, failing or giving poor grades, schools sometimes produce continued failure, rather than get students to succeed as they intend. (p. 1)

Consider the implications of this school policy: *Students who miss five days of class will receive a failing grade and no credit for the class.* For students who have good attendance, this policy may help to reinforce the importance of coming to class. But, for students who habitually miss school and have an established history of poor attendance, this policy probably will not be an effective motivator. These students are more likely to be overwhelmed by the new policy and simply give up. If additional supports do not accompany the policy, and are not put into place to assist students who already have a history of poor attendance, this policy may effectively push students who are at increased risk of school failure closer to that outcome. Efforts to improve educational outcomes by putting clear expectations in place are commendable. However, unintended consequences must be anticipated for those students who are already struggling and careful consideration given to strategies that can facilitate success for all students.

In addition to factors that push students out of school, many of the reasons students give for leaving school early are factors that *pull* students out of school. These factors compete with the goal of regular school attendance and successful completion as a first priority. These explanations for dropping out of school include having to care for family members, having peers who dropped out, having to work and go to school at the same time, and getting a job.

Using data from the National Educational Longitudinal Study of 1988, researchers found school-related push effects to be the most frequently reported reasons for dropping out. These were important predictors of the decision to drop out. This finding is actually somewhat encouraging, because it suggests that support personnel, educators, and administrators who work in schools can make a difference in whether students stay in school. The goal for school personnel who are trying to keep kids in school is to minimize the factors that tend to push students toward dropping out.

Data collected from large-scale studies also help to inform us about student explanations for dropping out of school. For example, using data from High School and Beyond, a national longitudinal study of nearly 30,000 high school students in the United States, researchers found several factors that differentiated students who dropped out of school from those who remained in school. Nearly 2,000 students who dropped out of school were asked their reasons for leaving (each student could choose as many reasons as applied). Reasons chosen by 10% or more of the students who dropped out included:

- Did not like school (33%)
- Poor grades (33%)
- Were offered a job and chose to work (19%)
- Getting married (18%)
- Could not get along with teachers (15%)
- Had to help support family (11%)
- Pregnancy (11%)
- Expelled or suspended (10%)

This national study helped educators and policymakers begin to focus on ways to address the problem. For example, one of the reasons students gave for dropping out was poor grades. A simplistic interpretation of this finding might imply that more students will remain in school if grades are substantially inflated. This does not get at the root cause of the problem. Rather than simply raising or inflating student grades, the reason why students are getting poor grades must be considered further. For example, are students getting poor grades because they are not motivated to do well, is the instruction relevant and engaging, can students retake exams until they have mastered material, is reteaching available, what is the quality of instruction? Answers to these questions help to inform an appropriate solution that will improve students' skills as well as their grades.

One way to determine the real reason for a problem is to look at the findings and ask "but why" a number of times before deciding that you have identified the root cause of the problem. In the Total Quality Management (TQM) model, this method is called "The Five Whys." Suppose you collected data and found that the highest proportion of students in your district dropped out in ninth grade. The next question to ask is why this occurred. If you were to apply the Five Whys you might discover that the root cause of the problem that appears in the ninth grade is that students do not have the basic reading skills needed to keep up with their coursework, so they drop out. With this knowledge, instead of trying to fix something in the ninth grade, a school could focus its attention on the need for students at the middle school level to increase their reading skills. Figure 4.1 illustrates the steps in this process.

Some school districts keep track of the number and percentage of students who drop out according to a list of designated reasons. For example, Table 4.2 shows the reasons for dropout and their definitions used by the Virginia Department of Education. With this kind of information, it is possible to identify reasons associated

Figure 4.1   Example of Key Finding Analysis Process: The Five Whys

The majority of students drop out in the ninth grade.	
1. But Why?	1. Students had to repeat ninth grade. (Permanent records of students)
2. But Why?	2. Students failed the majority of ninth grade courses. (Student transcripts)
3. But Why?	3. Students are unable to keep up with content reading required in ninth grade courses. (Student achievement test scores in fluency; student checklists; student interviews)
4. But Why?	4. Students possess weak reading fluency and comprehension skills. (Student permanent records; student achievement test scores)
5. But Why?	5. Students did not acquire basic reading skills in elementary school and did not receive remedial reading assistance in middle school. (Student permanent records; interview with middle school principal; review of middle school course offerings)

with the highest numbers of students leaving, determine areas to investigate further, and link to appropriate interventions. The information is even more helpful if it can be examined by student subgroups, such as ethnic, gender, and disability groups.

WHY STUDENTS STAY IN SCHOOL

Understanding why students stay in school is just as important as understanding why they drop out. If we understand what keeps kids in school, we can work to create those conditions. Theorists suggest that students are more likely to stay in school if they feel that they belong (see Box 4.2). When students feel that they are members of the school community, they are more likely to participate in school. Participation in school can

Table 4.2   Virginia Department of Education Reasons for Dropout

Dropout Reasons	Description
Achievement	Low achievement, low motivation, low interest, etc.
Behavioral Difficulties	Suspension or expulsion, incarceration, runaway, truancy, poor relationships with peers or adults, etc.
Employment	Took a job, joined the armed forces, entered Job Corps or similar program, etc.
Family	Pregnancy, parenthood, marriage, needed at home, etc.
Financial Hardship	Extreme poverty, working to support self or family, etc.
Health Problems	Physical or mental illness, injury, substance abuse, etc.
Moved, Current Status Unknown	No longer resides in the area and current status is unknown after appropriate investigation by the attendance officer.

SOURCE: Virginia Department of Education, Office of Information Technology *Report of Dropouts Data Collection, 2001–2002 School Year.* Retrieved July 31, 2004, from http://www.pen.K12.va.us/VDOE/Publications/Dropouts/datacoll/Instructions.doc

---

Box 4.2   Research: Participation and Identification = School Completion

One of the most influential theorists to shape current thinking on dropout and school completion is Jeremy Finn. He emphasized the importance of a student's bonding with school. Specifically, in order for students to remain engaged in school and ultimately graduate, students must actively *participate* in school and have a feeling of *identification* with school.

Participation is characterized by involvement in school activities. Examples of participation include attending school, completing assignments, taking part in informal social activities, joining extracurricular clubs, or participating in school governance. Participation in school activities yields successful performance, which in turn create feelings of identification with the school. Students who have a sense of affiliation with school are more likely to remain engaged and complete school. Lack of identification results in a sense of alienation, disengagement, and dropping out. Several studies have specifically investigated and linked the constructs of participation and identification with positive school outcomes including successful school completion (Finn, 1993).

---

take many forms. For example, students can participate by actively working on assignments in school, socializing with friends during lunch hour, or being involved in extracurricular activities, such as jazz band, theater productions, computer club, or sports. If students actively participate in school, they are more likely to feel successful and identify with their school. If students have a psychological or emotional connection with school, they are more likely to stay in school until they have graduated.

Larry Kortering and his colleagues have conducted some of the work on determining why students drop out of or stay in school. They have conducted hundreds of interviews and distributed thousands of surveys to learn from students who have dropped out. Based on all this, they have identified four principles as key to keeping kids in school. The principles are listed in Box 4.3.

> **Box 4.3** Principles for Keeping Kids in School
>
> *Principle 1:* Students must have a reason to want to complete school. They must understand the relevance of graduation to their future.
>
> *Principle 2:* Students need and want access to an adult who will encourage them to stay in school and help them to succeed. This does not have to be a parent, and in many cases, students who are at risk of not graduating may not have a parent to fill this role.
>
> *Principle 3:* Students need to have skills necessary for succeeding in today's high schools—including knowledge of *how* to learn. Schools must provide strategies that promote success on today's measures of performance.
>
> *Principle 4:* Students who stay in school often have found a way to become engaged in the nonacademic side of school (sports, clubs, or other groups).
>
> SOURCE: Adapted from Kortering, L. (2004). School completion principles. *Impact: Feature Issue on Achieving Secondary Education and Transition Results for Students with Disabilities, 16*(3), 7. Minneapolis: Institute on Community Integration, University of Minnesota. Adapted with permission from the author and publisher.

DROPOUT: A PROCESS OF DISENGAGEMENT

Elementary Years: The Process Begins

Dropping out of school is a process that often begins early in a student's school career. Although we usually count the act of leaving school or dropping out as an isolated event, students show signs that they are disengaging from school as early as their elementary years. One retrospective study, which is highlighted in Box 4.4, used students' cumulative school records to determine how early students at risk of not completing school could be identified. Results showed that dropouts could be distinguished from graduates with 66% accuracy by the third grade using attendance data.

Studies like these suggest that interventions should begin early. While few intervention studies have specifically targeted school completion from elementary grades through to high school, there is research that suggests that enhancing school success in early grades has a positive impact on the likelihood of school completion. A study in Canada showed the indirect effect of an elementary school intervention targeting social skills on subsequent dropout (see Box 4.5). It is one of the few studies so far that actually measured effects of an intervention implemented in the elementary grades on enrollment status years later.

The early intervention studies addressing dropout that have been conducted point to several important key components:

- Interventions focus on factors shown to be linked to dropout, and that can be influenced by educators, such as attendance, behavior, academic performance.
- Interventions begin early, sometimes as early as preschool.
- Strategies are focused on student engagement.
- Interventions occur over time, usually months or years.
- Interventions involve a family or parent component.

Box 4.4   The Importance of Engaging Students Early

Byron Barrington and Bryan Hendricks conducted a study to determine whether various characteristics could be used to differentiate graduates from those students who did not complete school. The overall sample included 204 students, some of whom were graduated, dropped out, or continued in high school beyond the four years. Information for each student was obtained from school records beginning in first grade, and included data on absences, achievement test scores, IQ scores, number of failing grades, grade point averages, documented teacher comments, parent occupational status, number of schools attended, and special education status. Significant differences were evident between the student groups on several variables. Statistical analysis indicated that students who dropped out of school could be distinguished from those who graduated with relative accuracy using information on absences, achievement tests, and teacher comments as early as the third grade. For example, dropouts could be distinguished from graduates with 66% accuracy by the third grade using information on attendance. By the fifth grade, students who dropped out were absent twice as often as the students who graduated (on average), and by the ninth grade, students who dropped out were absent three times as often as the graduates. The authors concluded that dropout prevention programs should be implemented in the elementary grades and include a component that works with parents to encourage their support and involvement in their child's school and learning. (For more information, see Barrington & Hendricks, 1989.)

Box 4.5   The Impact of Early Intervention on Dropout

The purpose of this program was to reduce student disruptiveness in the elementary grades so that students were less likely to be held back (in grade) and drop out of school. The intervention included social skills training for boys who were identified as at risk based on teacher report measures of behavior. The boys met in small groups (along with peers who were identified as having good social skills) twice a week during school hours for two years. In addition, those who implemented the intervention met regularly with classroom teachers to talk with them, monitor student progress, and identify opportunities to reinforce positive behavior. The second component of the model included a curriculum for working with parents on management skills. Parents received training sessions in their homes focused on teaching skills such as setting appropriate behavioral expectations, recognizing problem behaviors, and using reinforcement. A study of effectiveness indicated that the program had an indirect effect on later dropout. Children who received the intervention were less disruptive than a control group (who did not receive the intervention) and were less likely to be held back in grade or receive special education services. Risk of dropout decreased by more than half for program participants and the odds of students dropping out in high school were four times higher for youth who had been retained. This study points to the indirect effect of an early intervention focused on social and behavioral skills and dropping out of school. (For more information, see Vitaro, Brendgen, & Tremblay, 1999.)

Transition Between Schools: A Critical Time

Although disengaging from school may begin early, a high proportion of students drop out during the transition between schools—for example, during the transition from middle school or junior high school to senior high school. Keeping students engaged in school and with learning is especially important during transitions between schools, a time that can be especially stressful for youth. Transition to high school often includes navigating a more complex school setting, interacting with large numbers of unfamiliar peers, and the expectation to function more independently.

Techniques that have been used to ease transitions include creating smaller learning environments and providing more consistency in peers, teachers, and space by organizing classrooms into smaller teams that are close to each other. Homeroom teachers also can assume more of an advisory or guidance role, including tracking attendance, following up with parents about any absences, and regularly exchanging information with the family. New students can be assigned to older peers who act as mentors and help allay fears or answer questions about school procedures and daily routines. Establishing welcoming activities, such as picnics, orientation, team-building activities, or parent meetings at the beginning of the school year can also help to create schools that are more engaging.

Once a Dropout, Not Always a Dropout

Dropping out of school is not necessarily permanent. Students may drop out of school for a period of time, and then drop back into school again. The study by Barrington and Hendricks reported in Box 4.4 found that approximately 50% of the students who did not graduate after four years of high school returned for a fifth year, and more than 60% of those who returned obtained a diploma during that year. Many students who drop out of school return to schools that have been designed to serve students at risk of school failure. These schools are often referred to as "alternative schools." One survey conducted in Minnesota showed that nearly 60% of students who were attending alternative schools had dropped out in the past.

Providing educational options that reengage students who have dropped out is critical. Effective alternative schools have characteristics that work to engage students in schools, including low student-to-teacher ratios that allow more individual attention and programming, lessons tailored to individual interests, help with personal problems, and the use of problem-solving approaches to address discipline. Because students who drop out of school may return at some point, it is essential to have programs that are designed to recover this population. Other techniques for recovering students may include offering General Education Development (GED) programs, adult basic education, online computer courses, independent study programs, and magnet or charter schools.

A FOCUS ON COMPLETING SCHOOL

Decreasing the rate at which students are dropping out of school requires building supports and putting interventions in place that promote school completion. Box 4.6 describes such an approach. An approach that focuses on school completion has implications for the type of interventions that are designed and implemented.

Box 4.6   A Focus on School Completion

An explanation of the concept of school completion in relation to dropout prevention has been developed by researchers. This quote illustrates the differences between the two concepts in terms of meaning, orientation, and implications for interventions:

> Conceptually, school completion encompasses more than preventing dropout. It is characterized by a strength-based orientation (vs. a deficit orientation), a comprehensive interface of systems (vs. a narrowly defined intervention), implementation over time (vs. implementation at a single period in time) and creating a person-environment fit (vs. a programmatic "one size fits all" orientation). School completion is oriented toward a longitudinal focus, whereby interventions aim to promote a "good" outcome, not simply prevent a "bad" outcome for students and society. (Christenson, Sinclair, Lehr, & Hurley, 2000)

Approaches With Limited Effectiveness

Examples of dropout prevention approaches that seem to have limited effectiveness are those that include components that are short term, punishment oriented, and not focused on engaging students once they are in school.

• *Short-Lived Approaches.* Having a single group meeting for students who have chronic truancy. Consequences of truancy are explained, but strategies are not built in to follow up with students and families after attending the meeting.

• *Punishment-Oriented Approaches.* A policy is instituted where a student's driver's license is taken away if he or she misses too many days of school.

• *Approaches Not Focused on Engaging Students in School.* A policy is instituted where parents have to attend school with their child if the student is absent without a valid excuse for a designated number of days.

Effective Approaches to Increase School Completion

Intervention models that focus on school completion include approaches with components that engage students, are strength based, occur over time, and involve a variety of contexts. These approaches help to build students' skills so that they are equipped to function successfully in school. The message that school is important to your future is communicated to students through the use of these kinds of approaches. Examples of these include:

• *Approaches Focused on Engaging Students.* Smaller schools combine academic curriculum with technical instruction in a particular occupational field.

• *Strength-Based Approaches.* A class is provided that focuses on interpersonal relations, building social supports, and preventing drug use—to improve school attendance and academic performance.

• *Approaches Matched to Student Needs.* Intensive interventions (such as counseling or tutoring) are provided to address individual needs and risk factors associated with dropout (such as mental health needs or academic performance) and are coordinated through a mentor who has established a trusting relationship with the student over time.

- *Long-Term Approaches.* A weekly, year-long program is provided that incorporates volunteer service experiences and classroom-based discussion focused on building competence and coping skills.

- *Approaches Involving Various Contexts.* A high school has been reorganized into smaller learning communities focused on redefining the role of the homeroom teacher and increased information exchange between the home and school.

Implementation Scenario: Understanding Why: Looking at the Reasons, the Process, and the Approach (November)

The district-level committee moved on to the next major step in the process: determining why students were dropping out of school. Committee members decided to brainstorm a list of possible reasons. The exercise revealed multiple ideas such as not liking school, pregnancy and parenting, getting too far behind in credits, failing grades, and limited family support for staying in school and doing well. Initially, the staff from the elementary school did not think that this discussion was relevant to their population of students. But, after further reflection and discussion, committee members found that many of the reasons were preceded by signs that students were beginning to disengage from school in the early grades. In addition, although some of the reasons seemed simple, it was noted that some of them masked deeper underlying reasons. These reasons seemed especially important in relation to thinking about possible intervention approaches. For example, when the committee considered why students did not like school, reasons included not getting along with peers, which led to a discussion of teasing, bullying, and fights in school—all of which reflected on the school climate. Several members suggested that students may not like school because they did not feel as though they were a part of the school—that there was nothing that interested them or engaged them beyond coming to classes (which they did not do well in anyway!).

The committee decided to delve further into the reasons why students were dropping out of school. A list of students who did not return to school from the previous year was generated, and a brief telephone interview was developed to determine reasons why they dropped out. Although finding these students was sometimes challenging, family members proved to be very helpful in providing information about how the student could be contacted. In addition, the committee decided to look for evidence about when students were showing signs of disengagement by examining available information such as discipline referrals, absences, pregnancies, and failing grades at different levels (Grades 1, 4, 7, 9, and 11). This information provided a clearer picture of data-based reasons why students were disengaging and dropping out of school.

SUMMARY

In this chapter we wanted to broaden your understanding of the process of dropping out. To do that, we examined reasons why students stay in school and why they leave school early. We looked at both push and pull effects. Using this framework, it is easy to see that school staff, parents, and community members can do something about some of the reasons the students drop out. It is also possible to think about conditions that can be created to increase the holding power of schools.

We also explored the concept of dropout as a process that often starts early. It is important to establish a solid connection and engage students early and during critical transition periods. It is also important to realize that students who drop out of school may return to school later, and that options should be available to reengage them in school. Using a positive, skill-building approach focused on promoting successful school completion is a good way to address the challenge of students dropping out. All of this considered within the context of your setting will help set the foundation for building a strong program to increase graduation rates and decrease dropout rates.

The topics we covered in this chapter showed why students drop out and how interventions can make a difference. Now check your knowledge of the Myth or Truth? statements from the beginning of the chapter (see Box 4.7 for answers).

Box 4.7   Myth or Truth? Answers

1. **Myth.** Competing forces outside of school such as getting a job or having a child to care for are the most frequently cited reasons for dropping out of school. *Explanation:* In a national study, the most frequently cited reasons were actually school related. These reasons included poor school performance (failing classes), not getting along with teachers, or being suspended from school. (See page 59.)

2. **Truth.** Students are more likely to stay in school when they participate in school and learning and identify with their school. *Explanation:* Researchers have shown that students who participate in school and have successful school experiences develop a sense of belonging and are more likely to complete school. (See pages 62–63.)

3. **Myth.** The decision to drop out of school often occurs suddenly, with little warning. *Explanation:* The decision to drop out of school is a process that begins early and is often preceded by indicators of early withdrawal such as poor grades, behavior problems, and truancy. (See pages 64–65.)

4. **Myth.** Most students who drop out of school never return, and do not obtain a diploma or equivalent degree. *Explanation:* Many students who drop out of school return to school at some point and obtain a diploma or equivalent degree. (See page 66.)

5. **Truth**. Strategies that engage children and youth in school and learning are the key to keeping kids in school and raising graduation rates. *Explanation:* A common thread running through dropout prevention programs that have shown evidence of effectiveness is the use of strategies that engage students in school and learning. (See page 67.)

REFLECTION QUESTIONS

1. Think about the reasons why students drop out of school. How do these compare with what you know about why students drop out of school in your setting? What are the most common explanations for dropping out based on your experiences?

2. Dropping out of school is a process that begins early. How does this fit with your understanding of dropout? At what age should dropout prevention begin and what form should it take?

3. What are the implications of approaching the problem of dropout using a framework that focuses on school completion? How would interventions that are designed to promote school completion differ from those used to decrease dropout?

FURTHER READING

Alexander, K. L., Entwisle, D. R., & Kabbani, N. S. (2001). The dropout process in life course perspective: Early risk factors at home and school. *Teachers College Record, 103*(5), 760–822.

Barrington, B. L., & Hendricks, B. (1989). Differentiating characteristics of high school graduates, dropouts, and nongraduates. *Journal of Educational Research, 89*(6), 309–319.

Christenson, S. L., Sinclair, M. F., Lehr, C. A., & Hurley, C. M. (2000). Promoting successful school completion. In K. M. Minke & G. C. Bear (Eds.), *Preventing school problems—promoting school success: Strategies and programs that work* (pp. 211–257). Bethesda, MD: National Association of School Psychologists.

Ekstrom, R. B., Goertz, M. E., Pollack, J. M., & Rock, D. A. (1986). Who drops out of high school and why? Findings from a national study. *Teachers College Record, 87*(3), 356–373.

Felner, R. D., Brand, S., Adan, A. M., Mulhall, P. F., Flowers, N., Sartain, B., & Du Buis, D. L. (1993). Restructuring the ecology of the school as an approach to prevention during school transitions: Longitudinal follow-ups and extensions of the School Transitional Environment Project (STEP). *Prevention in Human Services, 10*(2), 103–136.

Finn, J. D. (1993). *School engagement and students at risk.* Washington, DC: U.S. Department of Education, National Center for Educational Statistics.

Jordan, W. J., McPartland, J. M., & Lara, J. (1999). Rethinking the causes of high school dropout. *The Prevention Researcher, 6*(3), 1–4.

Kortering, L. (2004). School completion principles. *Impact, 16*(4), 7.

Lange, C. M., & Lehr, C. A. (1997). *At-risk students in second chance programs: Reasons for transfer and continued attendance* (Research Report 20). Minneapolis: University of Minnesota, Enrollment Options Project.

Lehr, C. A., Sinclair, M. F., & Christenson, S. (2004). Addressing student engagement and truancy prevention during elementary years. A replication study of the Check & Connect model. *Journal of Education for Students Placed at Risk, 9*(3), 281–300.

Rumberger, R. W. (1995). Dropping out of middle school: A multilevel analysis of students and schools. *American Educational Research Journal, 32*(3), 583–625.

Schwienhart, L. J., & Weikart, D. P. (1998). Why curriculum matters in early childhood education. *Educational Leadership, 55*(6), 57–60.

Vitaro, F., Brendgen, M., & Tremblay, R. E. (1999). Prevention of school dropout through the reduction of disruptive behaviors and school failure in elementary school. *Journal of School Psychology, 37*(2), 205–226.

Wehlage, G. G., Rutter, R. A., Smith, G. A., Lesko, N., & Fernandez, R. R. (1989). *Reducing the risk: Schools as communities of support.* Philadelphia: Falmer Press.

TAKING ACTION

This section is written for those of you who are ready to begin doing something to decrease the number of students dropping out of school. If you are interested in gathering more information related to topics discussed in this chapter, sample tools have been provided to assist you. Whether working as a group or individually, locating existing data and collecting information will help you to answer key questions, evaluate current efforts, or reflect on a course of action. Action Tools are provided in this section.

One of your first tasks is to determine why students (in your school, district, or state) are dropping out of school. Gathering this information can take many forms. For example, the information can be gathered based on existing reports, talking with students, or using checklists. Find out what information is already being collected about reasons for dropout in your setting. The tools in this section are not general school improvement surveys—they have been specifically designed to gather information that is directly related to why students have dropped out of school. Some of the tools have been designed to be used (and have been used) with students who have dropped out of school. Understanding the reasons why students are dropping out in your setting by getting information from the students themselves may lead to valuable insights that can assist you in making changes to improve graduation rates.

Depending on your circumstances, there are a number of directions you can go from here. To determine what your next move should be, we recommend that you read through the statements in the left-hand column of the Guide to Action Tools on page 73, identify your most immediate needs, and then use the Action Tool listed in the right-hand column to gather the information you need. It is important to remember that the Action Tools are sample forms that are provided to assist you in gathering and organizing data that will help you to make informed decisions about how to address dropout in your setting. The tools can be reproduced; however, they may need to be modified to meet the needs of your school or district. Be sure to check whether there are district or school policies or procedures that must be followed before proceeding with the activities you plan to carry out.

GUIDE TO ACTION TOOLS

What Do You Need to Know or Do?	Action Tool
Determine why students are dropping out of school using existing data sources	Action Tool 4.1: *Dropout Reasons Data Form*
Determine why students are dropping out of school using interviews with students	Action Tool 4.2: *Student Interview Guide*
Determine why students are dropping out of school using a student checklist	Action Tool 4.3: *Student Checklist*
Determine when students are disengaging from school	Action Tool 4.4: *Disengagement Identification Form*

ACTION TOOL 4.1   DROPOUT REASONS DATA FORM

Objective: To find and document existing information about reasons students are dropping out of school

Materials: University study; anecdotal reports from school staff such as counselors or the attendance clerk; or an end-of-the-year School Report Card. (When possible, seek out multiple sources of information and try to find sources that have collected information in an objective manner.)

Instructions:

1. Analyze the data sources and reports to determine reasons why students are dropping out of school.

2. Record the information on the Action Tool.

Follow-Up:

1. Examine the data collected, and consider whether the reasons are primarily pushing or pulling students out of school.

2. Determine whether additional information must be collected to provide a more comprehensive picture.

3. Is information collected or reported by student subgroups (such as age, gender, ethnicity, disability)? If not, is it possible to get this information? If so, look for patterns to determine similarities and differences between groups.

4. After reviewing the data, develop and record a Summary Statement.

School/District _____

ACTION TOOL 4.1   DROPOUT REASONS DATA FORM

Question: What do we know about why students are dropping out of school?

Reasons	Data Source and Year

Summary Statement:

ACTION TOOL 4.2   STUDENT INTERVIEW GUIDE

Objective: To determine reasons why students drop out of and return to school

Instructions:

1. Identify students to interview. These should be students who are not currently enrolled, or who have dropped out in the past (although they may have returned to school).

2. Get student and parent permission for interviews (if necessary).
   ▲ *If you decide to conduct interviews with students younger than 18, parent permission may also be required. Student consent may also be required. We recommend that you check district policy before interviewing students.*

3. Interview students.

Follow-Up:

1. Review interview responses.

2. Compile responses across students by question.

3. Group common responses together. Determine themes within the responses for each question.

4. Review responses and themes. What are the most common reasons students give for dropping out of school?

5. Do responses differ by subgroup (such as age, gender, ethnicity, disability)? Look for patterns to determine similarities and differences between groups.

Source: Lehr, C. A. (1999). *At-risk students attending high schools: Factors that differentiate between persisters and dropouts.* Unpublished doctoral dissertation, University of Minnesota. Adapted with permission.

School/District _____

ACTION TOOL 4.2   STUDENT INTERVIEW GUIDE

Introduction (*paraphrase or modify as needed*):

Hello my name is _____. I am interested in finding out about reasons students decide to drop out of school and reasons why they decide to come back to school. Most of the information about why students drop out has been reported by parents or teachers, or the information comes from surveys. But I think it is important to *talk* with students about their reasons, and that is why I am doing this interview.

▶ *Add a statement with regard to confidentiality that is appropriate to your setting and consistent with your school policies.*

Student Information

Name	Age	English Language Learner (Yes/No)
Gender	Ethnicity	Identified Disability (Yes/No)
Current or Previous School Attended		

Background

- Have you ever dropped out of school for three weeks or more (missed 15 or more consecutive days of school not due to illness)?
- How many separate times have you dropped out of school?
- What grade(s) were you in when you dropped out of school?

Reasons for Dropping Out

- Think about the time(s) when you left school. Why did you decide to drop out?
- How did the school try to help you stay in school? How did the school try to help with problems you were having inside or outside of school? Who helped? What did they do?
- What could have been done to make it possible for you to stay in school?
- Were there things or people outside of school that could have helped you to stay in school? What or who were they?
- What did you do after you left school? How did you spend your time?

Reasons for Returning to School (if applicable)

- Have you returned to school or continued your education?
- What did you do to continue your education?
- Why did you decide to return to school or take classes again?
- How long after you dropped out of school did you first return to school or take classes?

Follow-Up

- What are you doing now?
- Are there things or people outside of school that help you to stay in school?
- Do you plan to graduate or earn your GED or have you already done so?
- What advice would you give the school you dropped out of to help keep kids in school and to graduate?

Copyright © 2005 by Corwin Press. All rights reserved. Reprinted from *Graduation for All: A Practical Guide to Decreasing School Dropout*, by Camilla A. Lehr, Ann T. Clapper, and Martha L. Thurlow. Thousand Oaks, CA: Corwin Press, www.corwinpress.com. Reproduction authorized only for the local school site or nonprofit organization that has purchased this book.

77

ACTION TOOL 4.3   STUDENT CHECKLIST

Objective: To determine reasons why students drop out of school

Instructions:

1. Identify students to survey. These students should be students who are not currently enrolled, or who have dropped out in the past (although they may have returned to school).

2. Get student and parent permission for administering surveys (if necessary).
   ▲ *If you decide to survey students younger than 18, parent permission may be required. Student consent may also be required. We recommend that you check district policy before interviewing students.*

3. Survey students.

Follow-Up:

1. Count the number of students choosing each response.

2. Review responses. What are the most common reasons?

3. Do responses differ by student subgroup (such as age, gender, ethnicity, disability)? Look for patterns to determine similarities and differences between groups.

Source: Lehr, C. A. (1999). *At-risk students attending high schools: Factors that differentiate between persisters and dropouts.* Unpublished doctoral dissertation, University of Minnesota. Adapted with permission.

School/District _____

ACTION TOOL 4.3   STUDENT CHECKLIST

Introduction (*paraphrase or modify as needed*):

This is a checklist that asks about reasons students decide to drop out of school and reasons why they decide to come back to school. There are no right or wrong answers.

Confidentiality Statement

▲ *Add a statement with regard to confidentiality that is appropriate to your setting and consistent with your school policies.*

Directions:

Think about the time(s) when you left school. Why did you decide to drop out? *Circle* the letter beside each statement in the column on the left that is a reason why you dropped out of school. Then think about why you returned to school and *circle* the letter beside each statement in the column on the right that influenced your decision to return. Before you begin, please complete the section on student information.

Student Information

Name	Age	English Language Learner (Yes/No)
Gender	Ethnicity	Identified Disability (Yes/No)
Current or Previous School Attended		

1. Why did you drop out of school?

a. I did not care about school and was not motivated
b. I had to care for a member of my family
c. I was pregnant
d. I thought the classes were boring
e. I wanted to travel
f. I had a drug or alcohol problem
g. I became the father/mother of a baby
h. I was getting poor grades/failing school
i. I got a job
j. I did not get along with other students
k. I had health problems
l. I did not feel safe at school
m. My friends had dropped out of school
n. I felt I did not belong at school
o. I could not keep up with my school assignments and homework
p. I had to support my family
q. I did not like school or the school environment
r. I was suspended or expelled from school
s. I did not get along with my teachers
t. Other _____
u. Other _____
v. Other _____

2. Why did you decide to return to school? What influenced your decision to return to school?

a. My parents expected me to graduate
b. I got some of my money problems solved
c. I got day care for my child
d. I got my family responsibilities under control
e. I got my drug/alcohol problem under control
f. I was more motivated and was interested in trying again
g. I got my behavior under control
h. I wanted to be with my friends
i. I was more confident
j. I thought that I could get along better with teachers
k. I thought I could get along with students at this school
l. I thought this school had better rules
m. I wanted a school that had smaller class sizes
n. I wanted a school that made me feel safer
o. I wanted a school that had a flexible schedule
p. I was encouraged to return by a staff member at this school
q. I recognized my responsibility as a parent to complete school
r. I wanted to graduate and get a diploma
s. I could get special education services to help me be successful in school
t. Other _____
u. Other _____
v. Other _____

ACTION TOOL 4.4   DISENGAGEMENT IDENTIFICATION FORM

Objective: To determine the extent to which students are showing signs of disengaging from school

Materials: Various data sources such as computerized lists of attendance by grade level, office discipline referrals, and report cards

Instructions:

1. Locate the data sources and reports that can be used to determine the extent to which students are disengaging from school.

2. Determine the grade levels for which you will be finding information. This Action Tool can be used with students in kindergarten through 12th grade, although some of the categories may not be applicable for all grade levels (such as teen pregnancy).

3. Record the unit of measurement that is being used for each risk factor. For example, the information on absences may be provided in number of days absent per quarter, total number of days absent the previous year, average percentage daily attendance, and so on.

4. Record the information collected.

Follow-Up:

1. Examine the data collected, and look for themes within grade levels and across grade levels.

2. Determine whether additional information must be collected to provide a more comprehensive picture.

3. If possible, disaggregate the information by subgroup to determine additional patterns (such as gender, disability, ethnicity).

4. After reviewing the data, develop and record a Summary Statement.

School/District _____

ACTION TOOL 4.4   DISENGAGEMENT IDENTIFICATION FORM

Question: To what extent are we seeing signs of disengagement in students by grade level?

Risk Factor	Unit of Measurement	Grade Level	Grade Level	Grade Level	Grade Level
Discipline Referrals					
Detentions					
In-School Suspensions (ISS)					
Out-of-School Suspensions (OSS)					
Truancy					
Absences					
Skipping Class					
Failing Grades					
Incompletes					
Behind in Credits					
Retention					
Teen Pregnancy					
Summary Statement:					

5

Considering What to Work On

Contextual Influences and Indicators

TOPICS

- Factors Placing Students at Risk of Dropping Out
- Keeping Students on the Path Toward Graduation
- Indicators of Student Engagement

IN THIS CHAPTER, YOU WILL . . .

- Learn about factors associated with increased risk of dropout
- Distinguish between alterable and status variables
- Identify protective factors that help keep students in school
- Learn about psychological, behavioral, cognitive, and academic indicators of student engagement
- Examine what is happening in your setting

What really distinguishes students who graduate from high school from those who do not? Are there situational factors, student characteristics, or other variables that place some students at risk of dropping out? The answers to these questions can help identify students who may be more likely to leave school early, and if we do

Box 5.1   Myth or Truth? Do You Know?

Read each statement following and decide whether it is a myth or the truth.

1. Students who have multiple risk factors in their lives almost always drop out of school.

2. We can predict with incredible accuracy who will drop out of school.

3. Educators, parents, and community members can do little to influence the trajectory leading to dropout or graduation because so many risk factors are not amenable to change.

4. The presence of a caring adult in a child's life is one of the most powerful protective factors fostering resilience.

5. Engaging students in school and learning is a key ingredient in the recipe for successful school completion.

that, then resources and supports can be directed toward them and they will be more likely to stay on the path to graduation.

Before you read the chapter, try to identify the myths or truths in Box 5.1. Answers are provided at the end of the chapter so that you can check your knowledge.

FACTORS PLACING STUDENTS AT RISK OF DROPPING OUT

Research studies have identified factors that place students at risk of dropping out of school. Some risk factors are more amenable to change and are considered *alterable*. Other risk factors are more difficult to change and are referred to as *status* variables. Within these two broad categories, the variables can be grouped further according to whether they are community- or school-level, family-level, or student-level variables. Attending school in an urban setting is an example of a *community-level status variable* that has been associated with increased risk of dropout. Dropout rates in urban schools, where poor and minority students are often concentrated, typically exceed the national average. In a recent article, the Civil Rights Project at Harvard University reported that in the 47 largest school districts, which usually are located in urban centers, the average dropout rate is nearly twice the national average. While not all students who attend schools in urban settings drop out, a higher proportion of students who do drop out are from urban schools. Table 5.1 lists examples of the alterable and status variables by community, school, family, and student levels.

Factors That Are Difficult to Change

It is difficult to change status risk factors through prevention and intervention efforts. But, recognizing that these factors increase the risk of dropout can help you

Table 5.1 Examples of Variables Placing Students at Risk of Dropout

	Alterable	*Status*
Community	*Support services*: Expensive or not accessible to all students	*Region*: Urban settings
School	*School policies*: Frequent use of suspension for discipline *School climate*: Unsafe, punitive environment *Instruction*: Lack of relevant/engaging and challenging instruction for all students	*School size*: Large
Family	*Parenting*: Permissive parenting styles *Educational support*: Few educational resources or limited support for learning *Life events*: Increased levels of stress or presence of stressors	*Income*: Low *Ethnicity*: Hispanic or Native American *Mobility*: Multiple changes in schools *Sibling history*: Siblings who have already dropped out
Student	*School performance*: Failing grades, poor test scores *Behavior*: Disciplinary problems *Attendance*: High numbers of absences and tardies to school *Belonging*: Feelings of alienation and lack of connectedness *Attitudes:* Low motivation and external locus of control	*Age*: Older in relation to same-grade peers *Ability*: Low cognitive ability *Disability*: Students with emotional/behavioral disabilities

understand the challenges you are facing and lead to ideas about ways to support students who are faced with these challenges. For example, suppose you have many low-income students in one school, and you have found through surveys that they do not have many educational resources in their homes nor do they have many educational experiences outside of the home. Knowing about this can help you justify the need for a grant for laptop computers that can be used at home by students, for example. Or, you may find a way to provide opportunities for students to participate in enrichment experiences, such as attending a science museum at reduced prices. Although educators cannot typically impact circumstances such as family income, understanding status variables that place students at risk is useful when considering interventions.

Factors That Can Be Influenced

There are community-, school-, family-, and student-level variables that can be changed. Resources and assistance provided to students at risk of school failure and their families is a *community-level alterable variable*. For example, a community that provides accessible mental health services through a collaborative relationship with a school, and uses a sliding fee scale for low-income families, increases the chances

Box 5.2   Positive School Climate: An Alterable School Level Variable

Research suggests that characteristics of the school environment can affect the outcomes of absenteeism and dropout for all students, and especially youth at risk of school failure. A healthy supportive school climate is characterized by:

- Students who believe they can learn and are willing to learn
- Parents, students, and staff who are involved in the decisions affecting the school
- Equal treatment of students regardless of ethnicity and gender
- Appropriate student behavior in the school
- A supportive community that is actively involved in the school
- Parent and staff expectations that students will do well academically and will lead successful lives
- A principal who takes a leadership role in guiding the direction of the school and in creating a positive climate
- A clean, well-maintained school building
- Positive, caring, and respectful student interpersonal relations
- Positive, caring, and respectful student-teacher relations

SOURCE: Adapted from Haynes, N. M., Emmons, C., & Ben-Avie, M. (1997). School climate as a factor in student adjustment and achievement. *Journal of Educational and Psychological Consultation, 8*(3), 321–329. Adapted with permission, Lawrence Erlbaum Associates Inc.

that students and their families will receive necessary services. The school environment is an example of a *school-level alterable variable.* Schools with a positive climate, characterized by respectful and caring relationships, high expectations, and discipline policies that are perceived as fair have also been linked to higher rates of graduation and lower rates of dropout. Instruments have been developed to measure school climate, and feedback from students, parents, and staff can help to inform school climate improvement projects. Characteristics of a school that has a positive school climate are listed in Box 5.2.

One way of creating safe and healthy schools that keep students coming to school is by providing a variety of supports to foster positive student behavior. Positive behavioral supports for all students are a critical foundation from which to build healthy and effective school environments that foster learning. Behavioral expectations must be established, taught, and enforced in order to create a safe school where effective academic instruction can occur. Using ongoing school improvement processes that set measurable goals and objectives and monitor progress toward those goals is critical. The School-Wide Information System (SWIS) is an example of a Web-based information system that can be used to improve the behavior support in elementary, middle, and high schools. The purpose of SWIS is to provide school personnel with practical information to help make decisions about discipline. Good decision making is based on getting good information in an accurate and timely manner. For example, does your school or district collect information about the number of office referrals that occur on a quarterly basis? Knowing what issues are of concern, the location and possible motivation for misbehavior, as well as the number of referrals, can provide valuable insight about how to influence an alterable variable associated with dropout and keep kids in school. Figure 5.1 shows an example of a SWIS office discipline referral form.

Figure 5.1 Web-Based SWIS Referral Form Example

Office Referral Form

Name: _____

Date: _____   Time: _____

Teacher: _____

Grade: K 1 2 3 4 5 6 7 8

Referring Staff: _____

Location

☐ Playground   ☐ Library

☐ Cafeteria   ☐ Bathroom

☐ Hallway   ☐ Arrival/Dismissal

☐ Classroom   ☐ Other _____

Problem Behavior	Possible Motivation	Administrative Decision
Minor ☐ Inappropriate language ☐ Physical contact ☐ Defiance ☐ Disruption ☐ Property misuse ☐ Other _____ **Major** ☐ Abusive language ☐ Fighting/ physical aggression ☐ Overt defiance ☐ Harassment/ tease/ taunt ☐ Disruption Other _____	☐ Obtain peer attention ☐ Obtain adult attention ☐ Obtain items/activities ☐ Avoid peer(s) ☐ Avoid adult ☐ Avoid task or activity ☐ Don't know ☐ Other _____	☐ Loss of privilege ☐ Time in office ☐ Conference with student ☐ Parent contact ☐ Individualized instruction ☐ In-school suspension (____ hours/ days) ☐ Out of school suspension (____ days) ☐ Other _____

Others involved in incident: ☐ None   ☐ Peers   ☐ Staff   ☐ Teacher   ☐ Substitute   ☐ Unknown   ☐ Other

If peers were involved, list them _____

Other comments: _____

☐ I need to talk to the students' teacher   ☐ I need to talk to the administrator

Parent Signature: _____   Date: _____

All minors are filed with classroom teacher. Three minors equal a major.

SOURCE: Todd, A. W., Horner, R. H. (2004). Referral form examples. SWIS. Retrieved June 1, 2004, from http://www.swis.org. Reprinted with permission.

Parent support for learning has been linked with academic performance and successful school completion. Parents can provide support in two important ways: they can assist with academic support, and they can also provide motivational support to their children. Some studies suggest that motivational support for learning plays a key role in student success—and may be even more important than providing academic support such as helping with homework or various assignments. It is important for school staff and communities to communicate the message to parents about the important role they play in engaging their children in school and learning. Many of the effective interventions designed to reduce dropout have a parent or family component in place.

High numbers of absences are predictive of increased risk of dropping out of school—this is an example of a *student-level alterable variable*. This variable is considered alterable because parents, educators, and others can influence student attendance through prevention or intervention strategies and programs. Research has shown that attendance is one of the strongest alterable variables linked to students dropping out of school. Students who have low rates of attendance are less likely to do well academically and more likely to leave school without a diploma. Attendance is a variable that can be affected by implementing strategies to decrease absences. For example, assigning an adult who acts as a mentor to regularly check in with the student and deliver the message that daily school attendance is important is one way of addressing this risk factor.

Students Placed at Risk

Students who have risk factors present in their lives are not destined to drop out of school. The presence of these factors should not be used as a reason to give up on a student. A gene for dropping out of school has not been identified, and these factors are better viewed as contextual variables that increase a student's vulnerability for dropping out of school. Alterable and status variables *place* students at risk—students are not *innately* at risk. Understanding this distinction helps students, parents, educators, administrators, and policymakers see that the problem of dropout is not solved by "fixing" the child, but instead, by building skills and influencing the contextual factors associated with leaving school early.

Multiple Factors Increase Risk

The presence of one or two risk factors does not *guarantee* that a student will drop out of school. In fact, some students will have many risk factors present in their lives, and still they will complete school. Research has confirmed that we are not very good at predicting who will actually drop out of school based on the information we have on risk factors associated with dropout. That is, if students who have multiple risk factors are identified in ninth grade as potential dropouts and they are followed until the end of their senior year to determine how many have dropped out of school, our hit rate (students who actually drop out of school) will not be 100%. A study by a research firm that demonstrated this finding is described in Box 5.3.

Given that we cannot predict who will drop out, what good is all the research about factors associated with dropout? The research evidence that we have is very useful in screening for students who are at risk of dropout and targeting interventions toward them. Some strategies can be used to improve screening tools and the chances that interventions are reaching the students who are most in need. These strategies are listed in Box 5.4.

Box 5.3 Do We Really Know Who Will Drop Out of School?

A study conducted by Mathematica Policy Research, Inc., used data from an evaluation of the School Dropout Demonstration Assistance Program (SDDAP) to determine the degree to which risk factors accurately predicted who would drop out of school. The risk factors included 20 student characteristics or measures of past school performance correlated with dropping out of school. A score was constructed for each student using these risk factors and about 20 additional student characteristics. The researchers found that "commonly used risk factors are inefficient predictors of whether students drop out. In both the middle and high school samples, at-risk students identified by these risk factors are more likely to have remained in school two to three years later than to have dropped out" (p. iv). For example, only 15% of students dropped out who had one of these risk factors: high absenteeism or overage for grade (two of the strongest predictors of dropout identified in the literature). Using multiple risk factors increased the accuracy of the prediction to correctly identify 42% of the students who actually dropped out in high school. The researchers conclude, "If programs are to continue to combat dropping out by targeting services toward at-risk students, they must work hard to find efficient means of identifying future dropouts" (p. v). They suggest incorporating more information to increase the efficiency of prediction, including ecological characteristics, unobserved psychological factors, persistent characteristics that occur over time, and transitory events. (For more information, see Gleason & Dynarski, 1998.)

Box 5.4 Guidelines for Increasing the Utility of Screening for Dropout

Consider the intensity of the factor placing the student at risk. A student with a disability may be at increased risk of dropout; however, if the student is doing well academically, socially, and behaviorally and the additional support is meeting his or her needs, the student may be at minimal risk of dropout.

Consider the number of risk factors placing the student at risk. Students with multiple status and alterable risk factors are at greater risk (for example, student with a learning disability, who has a history of missing more than 15 days of school for the past three years, recently suspended, hanging out with friends who have dropped out, living in poverty with little home support for learning).

Consider the underlying contextual information. A student missed 15 days of school in one year because of one week of family vacation to Mexico, seven days due to chicken pox, and three other single days due to illness throughout the year. Attendance in previous years has been greater than 95%.

Consider whether risk factors are at the group or individual level. Attending an urban school is a group-level variable that carries less predictive value than a student's increasingly poor work completion and failing grades.

Consider whether both objective and subjective information is being utilized. Gathering teacher input or ratings of engagement in school or information about a persistent pattern of disengagement may provide valuable information in addition to objective data on attendance and grades.

Consider whether any protective factors are in place. An involved and caring parent who provides motivational support for learning can be a powerful protective factor to help keep a student in school.

Results from an integrative review of 45 interventions designed to prevent dropout indicated that youth who participated in the intervention programs were most often selected on the basis of poor academic performance, such as low grade point average or test scores, followed by poor attendance, including high numbers of absences and tardies, teacher referrals, and previous instances of dropping out of school. More than half of the studies selected participants based on two or more criteria. This practice is consistent with the research literature that suggests the presence of multiple risk factors increases the risk of dropout. Using multiple risk factors also increases the chances of correctly identifying students who are most in need of support for staying in school.

Perhaps your school or district already targets students who may be at risk of dropping out of school. Some schools screen for students who may be at risk of dropping out using computerized lists of attendance, teacher referrals, or team meetings. It is important to have some way of systematically identifying who may be in need of additional support to keep them on the path toward graduation. Figure 5.2 shows a sample form that was developed from the research literature and used to identify students for participation in Check & Connect, a model designed to engage students in school and prevent dropout.

KEEPING STUDENTS ON THE PATH TOWARD GRADUATION

What can educators, community members, and parents do to keep students on the path toward graduation? How do you know where to start and what to focus on? The good news is that the variables associated with increased risk of dropout can be used to choose appropriate interventions that will facilitate school completion!

Focusing on Alterable Variables to Promote School Completion

Earlier in this chapter, alterable variables associated with dropout were identified and categorized into community-, school-, family-, and student-level variables. These variables can be used to design or select interventions to address the reasons why students are dropping out. For example, poor academic performance as indicated by failing grades and low test scores is an alterable student-level variable that is a strong predictor of dropout. An intervention that focuses on strengthening academic skills can be a powerful intervention designed to address the needs of those students at risk of leaving school due to failing coursework.

Alterable variables are a source of hope for those who want to keep students on the path to school completion. For example, educators can influence academic performance through the use of instructional strategies, peer tutoring, and quality after-school programs. Community members can influence student motivation toward learning and school completion by initiating and participating in mentoring activities and work study programs. Parents can influence attendance by setting clear expectations, increasing communication between home and school, and monitoring absences. Identifying the risk factors associated with dropout and redefining them as goals and strategies that facilitate school completion is one of the keys to designing effective interventions. Table 5.2 illustrates how risk factors can be useful for determining goals and strategies to address those goals.

Figure 5.2   Check & Connect Elementary Referral Form

Most referrals are initially generated via student attendance records and reviewed by a team typically consisting of the principal, monitor, and other school staff identified by the principal.

Please Complete:

Student Name:	School:
Grade:	Teacher:
Date of Request:	

Critical Information For Referral

Number of absences during year _____ / number of days enrolled:	/
Number of tardies during year _____ / number of days enrolled:	/
Number of absences during year _____ / number of days enrolled:	/
Number of tardies during year _____ / number of days enrolled:	/

Supporting Information For Referral

If the student is tardy, indicate how late the student arrives on average (e.g., 5 to 10 minutes late or tends to miss the first two hours)	
Indicate parent(s)' level of involvement in child's education. Note major concerns:	☐ High ☐ Adequate ☐ Low
Does this student have siblings who have a history of excessive absences or who have dropped out?	☐ Yes ☐ No
Does this student have a sibling(s) who is in Check & Connect?	☐ Yes ☐ No
Does the child complete their homework or follow through on assignments that must be finished at home?	☐ Yes ☐ No
Is the student actively engaged in learning activities at school (e.g., participates in discussions, thinks school is important, attempts tasks with good effort, knows what is going on in class)?	☐ Yes ☐ No
Is the student receiving any additional services from within the school? (e.g., Title I, Special Education, etc.) Please list:	☐ Yes ☐ No

Please add any other pertinent information that could help to determine whether a referral to the Check & Connect program is appropriate.

Based on the above information, what is the referral's priority?   Hold   Low   High

Recommendations if not appropriate for Check & Connect:

SOURCE: Sinclair, M. F., Lehr, C. A.., Kaibel, C., & Christenson, S. L. (2001). Check & Connect referral form. University of Minnesota, Institute on Community Integration. Reprinted with permission.

Table 5.2   Alterable Risk Factors Transformed

*Alterable risk factors can be transformed into targeted goals that
will inform selected strategies or interventions that affect student outcomes.*

Risk Factor →	Goal →	Strategy →	Desired Outcome/ Protective Factor
Poor attendance	Increase rate of attendance	Strategies to increase attendance (e.g., better monitoring, increased home-school communication, daily check-in with the student)	Regular and high rates of attendance
Failing grades	Improve grades	Strategies to improve grades (e.g., tutoring sessions, reteaching, mastery orientation)	Passing grades

Protective Factors That Keep Kids in School

Why do some of the students who appear as though they are very likely to drop out actually remain in school and graduate? Several reasons have been suggested. One is that they are resilient. Even some youngsters who face the toughest of circumstances in their lives move beyond the challenges that surround them to become competent and productive citizens. Studies have identified protective factors that distinguish between high-risk children who ended up as successful adults and those who were not successful. A summary of these characteristics is presented in Table 5.3.

The contextual characteristics of resilient children and youth are particularly encouraging for those who are trying to keep at-risk students in school, particularly those at risk due to circumstance and ability! Resilient behaviors that can lead to school completion can be fostered through educational environments that provide access to positive and caring relationships with adults, encouraging participation in school extracurricular activities, and providing opportunities to develop academic, personal, and social competence. In an article on risk and resilience by Beth Doll and Mark Lyon, the authors emphasize the significant role that schools and educators can play in fostering resilience in youth:

> For those students who are at greatest risk due to accumulation of multiple risk factors, schools may represent one of the most potentially protective environments—encouraging the development of good problem-solving and academic skills, individual talents and other productive activities, and social competence. This implies of course, that educators view such activities as a fundamental part of the school's mission and that adults in the school environment are willing to establish stable and meaningful relationships with at-risk students. (p. 357)

Table 5.3   The Power of Resilience

Individual and Contextual
Characteristics of Resilient Children and Youth

Individual	*Contextual*
Good intellectual ability	**Family Related**
Language competence	Close, affectionate relationship with at least one parent or caregiver
Positive temperament or easygoing disposition	Effective parenting (characterized by warmth, structure, and high expectations)
Positive social orientation including close peer friendships	Access to warm relationships and guidance from other extended family members
High self-efficacy, self-confidence, and self-esteem	**School or Community Related**
Achievement orientation with high expectations	Access to and relationships with positive adult models in a variety of extrafamilial contexts, including schools
Resilient belief system, faith	
Higher rate of engagement in productive activities	Connections with at least one or a variety of prosocial organizations
	Access to responsive, high-quality schools

SOURCE: Doll, B., & Lyon, M. A. (1998). Risk and resilience: Implications for the delivery of educational and mental health services in schools. *School Psychology Review, 27*(3), 348–363. Copyright 1998 by the National Association of School Psychologists, Bethesda, MD. Reprinted with permission of the publisher.

The importance of early intervention in building competence and resilience is worth noting again. High-quality preschool programs for children with early family support services such as the Perry Preschool Project have been shown to enhance academic and social competence as well as prevent problem behaviors such as delinquency. Establishing a solid foundation by engaging children early in their school and providing skills so that they can successfully meet the demands of later schooling is a strong preventive approach that can be used to decrease dropout.

INDICATORS OF STUDENT ENGAGEMENT

Student engagement has been identified as a critical component of successful school completion. The degree to which students are engaged in school varies. Some students have good attendance, making it seem like they are engaged in school even though they do not have a strong affiliation or sense of pride in their school. Other students may not do well in basic academic courses, such as English or math, but may enjoy and be very successful in other classes such as art or woodworking. Still other students may be engaged in school through involvement in extracurricular activities such as sports or student council (see Box 5.5). All of these students are engaged to some degree and are more likely to leave school with a diploma than those who are not engaged.

Clearly, student engagement in school can take many forms. The stronger the connection to school, the greater the chance of completing school and obtaining a diploma. A student who has a strong bond with school (like superglue) can be

---

Box 5.5   The Power of Involvement in Extracurricular Activities

---

Researchers Joseph Mahoney and Robert Cairns conducted a study to determine whether extracurricular activities protect against early school dropout. Interviews were conducted annually for six years with nearly 400 youth (starting in Grade 7). Participation in activities was compared across Grades 7 to 10 for dropouts and nondropouts. Students who dropped out of school participated in significantly fewer extracurricular activities across all grades. Students who were categorized as at risk but who engaged in any extracurricular activity during Grades 7 through 10 graduated from high school. The researchers hypothesized that for students whose prior commitment to the school was marginal, participation in extracurricular activities provided an opportunity to create a positive and voluntary connection to school. In light of the results, exclusionary policies characteristic of some schools with regard to participation in activities may work against those students who could benefit most directly from the involvement. (For more information, see Mahoney & Cairns, 1997.)

---

characterized as highly engaged. Typically, these students are successful—doing well academically (get good grades) and behaviorally (well liked, good social skills)—enjoy coming to school, feel comfortable with students and teachers, and feel competent in meeting the demands of the school environment. A student who has a weak connection with school (hanging by a thread) may be failing several classes, attend sporadically, have few friends, and feel minimal support from teachers.

The concept of engagement is complex. Sandy Christenson, a professor and researcher at the University of Minnesota, has explored the construct of student engagement and has identified four dimensions: *psychological* (belonging, identification with school), *behavioral* (attendance, classroom participation), *cognitive* (self-regulated learning), and *academic* (time on task, homework completion) engagement. Box 5.6 lists the four dimensions of engagement along with brief explanations and examples of each.

Although the dimensions can be described separately, distinctions actually blur across dimensions. Still, the framework helps illustrate the multidimensional nature of engagement. It also points to possible strategies that can be used to influence specific dimensions of engagement. More research is needed to make comprehensive statements about the role of each dimension on overall student engagement and its specific contribution to school completion.

Implementation Scenario: Considering What to Work On: Contextual Influences and Indicators (December)

Although the committee had a clearer idea of why students were dropping out of school and when signs of disengagement were occurring, they also believed it was important to identify students who were particularly at risk of dropping out of school. Initial discussion focused on risk factors such as coming from a background of poverty and stressful family situations. After doing some background reading, committee members realized that many factors placing students at risk of dropout have been identified through research and categorized into those that are relatively stable and those that can be more easily influenced. Using established checklists, the committee members identified status variables and alterable variables at the

> **Box 5.6   Examples: Indicators of Student Engagement**
>
> **Academic Engagement** may be reflected in the amount of time a student is actually doing school work or related projects in school or at home, the number of credits the student has accrued, or the amount of homework completed.
>
> **Behavioral Engagement** is reflected in student behavior. For example, students who are behaviorally engaged are physically present as indicated by high rates of attendance, active participation in class (asking questions, participating in discussions), or involvement in extracurricular activities.
>
> **Cognitive Engagement** refers to the extent to which a student's internal thought processes are focused on school and learning. A student who is cognitively engaged is a student who has good problem-solving skills and sees the relevance of school to future aspirations. Students who are cognitively engaged show interest in learning and go a step beyond to process and apply what is taught.
>
> **Psychological Engagement** refers to a student's emotional or psychological connection to school and learning. Students who are psychologically engaged feel that they belong and are a part of the school community. They identify as members of the school and may show this by supporting their school in a variety of ways.

community, school, family, and student levels. Based on available evidence, each risk variable was rated according to its intensity and degree of impact on disengagement and dropout. To some committee members' surprise, many of the factors placing students at risk were actually ones that they thought could be affected by educators, community members, and families working together.

Committee members were struck by the high intensity ratings in the area of school-level variables—both status (for example, large schools with large class sizes) and alterable (degree to which the school was perceived as welcoming). Feedback from parents and students on the annual district survey indicated concern in the area of school climate, safety, and respect between peers as well as between students and teachers, especially in the middle school. Records also showed a high number of absences and average daily attendance of less than 85% at the high school. Interestingly, there was also a core group of students in elementary school with absences greater than 15 over a period of two years. This information led to a discussion of discipline and attendance policies. In addition to looking at district board policies, each of the pilot schools studied their respective handbooks to evaluate and update policies in light of their impact on student engagement in school and graduation.

SUMMARY

In this chapter we moved beyond Chapter 4's conceptual understanding of the problem of dropout. Now we are thinking about what to work on to increase rates of school completion. We looked at information about factors that place students at risk of dropout, and we distinguished between the kinds of factors that are amenable to change through prevention or intervention efforts (alterable variables) and those that are more difficult to influence (status variables). Knowledge of the kinds of alterable variables that are associated with dropout is helpful because they can be used to design strategies to address what is placing the student at risk of dropping out.

In this chapter we also identified protective factors that help to keep students in school and contextual characteristics fostering resilient children and youth. Knowing what works to build competence and keep kids in school can guide you in creating the necessary supports in schools and communities. We concluded by noting that student engagement is a multidimensional construct that provides clues about how to engage students academically, behaviorally, psychologically, and cognitively. If students are engaged in school, they are much more likely to remain in school and obtain a diploma.

Now check your knowledge of the Myth or Truth statements from the beginning of the chapter (see Box 5.7 for answers). How did you do?

Box 5.7   Myth or Truth? Answers

1. **Myth.** Students who have multiple risk factors in their lives almost always drop out of school. *Explanation:* Although the presence of multiple risk factors in students' lives increases the likelihood of dropping out of school, many students who have multiple risk factors in their lives do in fact complete school! (See pages 87–88.)

2. **Myth.** We can predict with incredible accuracy who will drop out of school. *Explanation:* Researchers have shown through longitudinal studies that we cannot predict who will drop out of school with certainty. However, use of multiple risk factors increases the accuracy of our predictions. (See pages 87–88.)

3. **Myth.** Educators, parents, and community members can do little to influence the trajectory leading to dropout or graduation because so many risk factors are not amenable to change. *Explanation:* Many factors associated with dropout are amenable to change through prevention or intervention including attendance, academic performance, and behavior. Educators, parents, and community members can influence these variables. (See page 89.)

4. **Truth.** The presence of a caring adult in a child's life is one of the most powerful protective factors fostering resilience. *Explanation:* Research has shown that children who have a caring adult in their lives are more likely to have healthy adjustment despite the presence of multiple factors placing them at risk. (See page 91.)

5. **Truth.** Engaging students in school and learning is a key ingredient in the recipe for successful school completion. *Explanation:* Engaging students is one of the most important keys to successful school completion and is a recurring theme in successful programs and interventions designed to prevent dropout. (See pages 92–93.)

REFLECTION QUESTIONS

1. Choose one alterable variable and one status variable associated with the risk of dropping out of school. For example, you might choose attendance as an alterable variable and urban setting as your status variable. Brainstorm strategies to reduce the level of risk and discuss the degree of influence educators can have on addressing the problem of dropout.

2. Refer to the discussion in this chapter of protective factors linked with competence and resilience. How could these be operationalized in school and community settings?

3. Think about the explanation of psychological, behavioral, cognitive, and academic indicators of engagement. What strategies can be used to engage students in each of these ways?

FURTHER READING

Bempechat, J. (1998). *Against the odds: How "at-risk" students EXCEED expectations.* San Francisco: Jossey-Bass.

Christenson, S. L., & Sheridan, S. M. (2001). *School and families: Creating essential connections for learning.* New York: Guilford.

Christenson, S. L., Sinclair, M. F., Lehr, C. A., & Hurley, C. M. (2000). Promoting successful school completion. In K. M. Minke & G. C. Bear (Eds.), *Preventing school problems— Promoting school success: Strategies and programs that work* (pp. 211–257). Bethesda, MD: National Association of School Psychologists.

Christenson, S. L., & Thurlow, M. L. (2004). School dropouts: Prevention considerations, interventions, and challenges. *Current Directions in Psychological Science,13*(1), 36–39.

Civil Rights Project. (2004). *Dropouts: Keeping students in school.* Civil Rights in Brief, Harvard University. Retrieved July 23, 2004, from http://www.law.harvard.edu/civilrights

Doll, B., & Lyon, M. A. (1998). Risk and resilience: Implications for the delivery of educational and mental health services in schools. *School Psychology Review, 27*(3), 348–363.

Dynarski, M., & Gleason, P. (1999). *How can we help? Lessons from federal dropout prevention programs.* Princeton, NJ: Mathematica Policy Research.

Finn, J. D. (1993). *School engagement and students at risk.* Washington, DC: U.S. Department of Education, National Center for Educational Statistics.

Gleason, P., & Dynarski, M. (1998). *Do we know whom to serve? Issues in using risk factors to identify dropouts.* Princeton, NJ: Mathematica Policy Research.

Haynes, N. M., Emmons, C., & Ben-Avie, M. (1997). School climate as a factor in student adjustment and achievement. *Journal of Educational Psychological Consultation, 8*(3), 321–329.

Lehr, C. A., & Christenson, S. L. (2002). Promoting a positive school climate. In A. Thomas & J. Grimes (Eds.), *Best practices in school psychology IV.* Bethesda, MD: National Association of School Psychologists.

Mahoney, J., & Cairns, R. (1997). Do extracurricular activities protect against early school dropout? *Developmental Psychology, 33*(2), 241–253.

Masten, A. S., & Coatsworth, J. D. (1998). The development of competence in favorable and unfavorable environments. *American Psychologist, 53*(2), 205–220.

Morse, A. B., Anderson, A. R., Christenson, S. L., & Lehr, C. A. (2004). Promoting school completion. *Principal Leadership, 4*(6), 9–13.

Rosenthal, B. S. (1998). Non-school correlates of dropout: An integrative review of the literature. *Children and Youth Services Review, 20*(5), 413–433.

Rumberger, R. W. (1995). Dropping out of middle school: A multilevel analysis of students and schools. *American Educational Research Journal, 32*(3), 583–625.

Sugai, G., Sprague, J. R., Horner, R. H., & Walker, H. M. (2000). Preventing school violence: The use of office discipline referrals to assess and monitor school-wide discipline interventions. *Journal of Emotional and Behavioral Disorders, 8*, 94–101.

TAKING ACTION

This section is for those of you who are working in groups or individually, who are ready to begin doing something to decrease the number of students dropping out of school. But, this will require taking some action to gather information that will assist you in your decision making. One of the first things you will need to do after reading this chapter is to identify status and alterable variables placing students at risk in your setting. Gathering this information will help provide insight about the type of intervention that is necessary to impact rates of graduation. In this section, sample forms are provided that can be used to document information about factors placing students at risk of dropout in your setting. The key is to identify information that is already collected or resources that can be used to gather the information. For example, if you are trying to find out about attendance, possible sources of information may include the attendance clerk, a computerized printout of attendance at the school level, or data compiled by the district. It may also be to helpful to review policies that are already in place to see what impact these have on promoting school completion. Tools that can be used to help organize information and review school board policies and parent, student, or teacher handbooks are included here.

Depending on your circumstances, there are a number of directions you can go from here. To determine what your next move should be, we recommend that you read through the statements in the left-hand column of the Guide to Action Tools on page 99, identify your most immediate needs, and then use the Action Tool listed in the right-hand column to gather the information you need. It is important to remember that the Action Tools are sample forms that are provided to assist you in gathering and organizing data that will help you to make informed decisions about how to address dropout in your setting. The tools can be reproduced, however, they may need to be modified to meet the needs of your school or district. Be sure to check whether there are district or school policies or procedures that must be followed before proceeding with the activities you plan to carry out.

GUIDE TO ACTION TOOLS

What Do You Need to Know or Do?	Action Tool
Identify status variables placing students at risk	Action Tool 5.1: *Status Variables Checklist*
Identify alterable variables placing students at risk	Action Tool 5.2: *Alterable Variables Checklist*
Determine how existing school board policies impact student engagement and school completion	Action Tool 5.3: *Board Policy Analysis Form*
Determine how existing policies found in student, parent, or teacher handbooks impact school completion	Action Tool 5.4: *Handbook Analysis Form (Student, Parent, Teacher)*

ACTION TOOL 5.1   STATUS VARIABLES CHECKLIST

Objective: To determine status variables contributing to student risk of dropout

Instructions:

1. Review status risk factors at the community, school, family, and student levels. These variables are associated with dropout and are difficult to influence or change. Many are listed in the Status Variables Checklist; however, it may be necessary to generate others that are relevant to your setting.

2. Gather and document evidence to determine intensity of risk variable.

3. Rate intensity of risk variable in your setting. For example, suppose a high school has a large enrollment of more than 2,000 students in Grades 9–12. However, the school is organized into smaller learning communities. This suggests the intensity of the risk factor is less because it has been addressed to limit its impact.

Follow-Up:

1. Review risk factors with the highest ratings in your setting.

2. Consider whether and how these factors are impacting student rates of dropout.

3. Determine whether and how these risks are being addressed.

4. Develop a Summary Statement and discuss action steps for risk factors that are not being addressed.

School/District _____

ACTION TOOL 5.1   STATUS VARIABLES CHECKLIST

Status Variables	Evidence	Intensity Rating		
		Low	Medium	High
Community Level				
Urban Community				
High Level of Poverty				
Other				
School Level				
Large Enrollment				
Limited Resources (e.g., textbooks)				
Other				
Family Level				
Homeless				
Parents With Limited Education				
Non-English Speaking				
High Mobility (Frequently moving)				
Low Income				
Limited Educational Resources				
Other				
Student Level				
A Disability				
History of Sibling Dropout				
Other				
Summary Statement:				

101

ACTION TOOL 5.2   ALTERABLE VARIABLES CHECKLIST

Objective: To determine alterable variables contributing to student risk of dropout

Instructions:

1. Review alterable risk factors at the community, school, family, and student levels. These variables are associated with dropout and are more amenable to change. Many are listed in the Alterable Variables Checklist, however, it may be necessary to generate others that are relevant to your setting.

2. Gather and document evidence to determine intensity of risk variable.

3. Rate intensity of risk variable in your setting. Suppose your school is in a rural community, and very few community activities are available for youth. However, nearly all of the youth are involved in the 4-H opportunities that are offered throughout the year. The intensity of this rating may fall in the low range, because the majority of the youth are involved in the opportunity that is available.

Follow-Up:

1. Review risk factors with the highest ratings in your setting.
2. Consider whether and how these factors are impacting student rates of dropout.
3. Determine whether and how these risks are being addressed.
4. Develop a Summary Statement and discuss action steps for risk factors that are not being addressed.

School/District _____

ACTION TOOL 5.2   ALTERABLE VARIABLES CHECKLIST

Alterable Variables	Evidence	Intensity Rating		
		Low	Medium	High
Community Level				
Limited Supports for Basic Needs				
Limited Community Activities for Youth				
Other				
School Level				
Poor School Climate				
Punitive Policies (Frequent suspension)				
Unsafe School Environment				
Other				
Family Level				
Limited Involvement in Child's Schooling				
Permissive Parenting Style				
Other				
Student Level				
Behind in Credits				
Poor Attendance (Number of absences)				
Retained/Overage for Grade				
Behavior or Discipline Referrals				
Chemically Dependent				
Other				
Summary Statement:				

ACTION TOOL 5.3   BOARD POLICY ANALYSIS FORM

Objective: To review and analyze board polices to determine the extent to which they engage students and positively impact school completion

Materials: Board policies in these areas: attendance, truancy, discipline, provision of positive behavioral supports, suspension, grading, retention, tracking, failing grades, zero tolerance, opportunities to earn credit, corporal punishment, student rights and responsibilities, dropout

Instructions:

1. Document board polices on the Action Tool.

2. Review the policies with regard to their impact on school completion, then rate them with 1 = negative impact to 5 = positive impact.

Follow-Up:

1. Analyze responses and discuss your findings in relation to the following questions:
   Do these policies foster resilience or act as protective factors?
   Do these policies push or pull students out of school?
   Do these policies help to engage or disengage children and youth?
   To what degree are the policies implemented consistently?

2. Develop a statement summarizing your findings.

School/District _____

ACTION TOOL 5.3   BOARD POLICY ANALYSIS FORM

Policy Area	Existing Language	Impact on School Completion (1) Negative to Positive (5)					
Example: Suspension and Expulsion Guidelines	*Example: Pupil suspension length varies according to the severity of misconduct. Truancy results in up to a maximum of 3 days suspension.*	X					
Summary Statement:							

ACTION TOOL 5.4 HANDBOOK ANALYSIS FORM (STUDENT, PARENT, TEACHER)

Objective: To review and analyze written guidelines and procedures as documented in student, parent, or teacher handbooks to determine the extent to which they engage students and positively impact school completion

Materials: *Student handbooks* with guidelines and procedures on discipline, code of conduct, attendance, consequences for truancy, grading, harassment/bullying; *Parent handbooks* with guidelines and procedures on school/community resources, parenting support (management, homework, parenting styles), home-school communication, student discipline procedures, conferences, attendance, grading, opportunities for involvement; *Teacher handbooks* with guidelines and procedures on disciplinary approach, parent communication, parental notification of absences, failing grades, behavioral problems, assignment completion and missing work, grading, and attendance

Instructions:

1. Document guidelines and policies on the Action Tool that is provided.

2. Review the policies with regard to their impact on school completion, then rate them with 1 = negative impact to 5 = positive impact.

Follow-Up:

1. Analyze responses and discuss your findings in relation to the following questions:

   Do these policies foster resilience or act as protective factors?

   Do these policies push or pull students out of school? Do these policies help to engage or disengage children and youth?

   Do these policies help to engage parents in their child's school and learning?

   To what degree are the policies implemented consistently?

2. Develop a statement summarizing your findings.

106

School/District _____

ACTION TOOL 5.4   HANDBOOK ANALYSIS FORM (Student, Parent, Teacher)

Title of Handbook (Student, Parent, or Teacher) _____

Policy or Guideline	Existing Language	Impact on School Completion (1) Negative to Positive (5)				
		1	2	3	4	5
Example: Attendance	*Example: If a student is going to miss school, the parent is responsible for calling the attendance clerk to indicate the reason for the absence. If no call is made before 9:00 a.m. on that day, the school attendance clerk will follow up.*				X	
Summary Statement:						

6

Clarifying the Focus

Prevention and Intervention Programs

TOPICS

- Prerequisites: Establishing a Solid Foundation
- Types and Examples of Interventions
- Linking the Intervention to Identified Needs
- Levels of Intervention

IN THIS CHAPTER, YOU WILL . . .

- Consider the role early intervention and effective schools play in relation to school completion
- Learn about types of interventions that have been used to prevent dropout
- Examine strategies and interventions that engage students in school and learning
- Consider the importance of linking strategies with identified needs
- Identify three levels of intervention

So what really works to engage students in school and learning, complete school successfully, and leave with a diploma? This chapter begins with a brief overview of the importance of early intervention and effective schools in relation to establishing a sound foundation for successful school completion. Next, examples of the kinds of interventions that have some evidence of their effectiveness are provided. We also talk about approaches geared to large numbers of students at the systems level

---

Box 6.1   Myth or Truth? Do You Know?

Read each statement following and decide whether it is a myth or the truth.

1. The most effective strategy for addressing the problem of dropout has been clearly identified, is well researched, and has been replicated in multiple settings.

2. Most interventions that have been systematically reviewed use multiple strategies to address the problem of dropout.

3. Interventions that include a family outreach component are the most commonly used means of addressing dropout.

4. Universal interventions are a useful preventive approach for promoting school completion and typically target a large percentage of students.

5. It is nearly impossible to provide interventions across all three levels (universal, selected, and indicated) and effectively address the needs of students in general and those at risk of school failure.

---

that can be used to enhance the chances of engaging students, improving student behavior, and increasing academic performance, and that subsequently result in higher graduation rates. Approaches that are clearly geared to students who are at high risk of leaving school early are highlighted, as well as a variety of ways to address dropout that have been used effectively in other settings.

Before going further, test your knowledge by identifying this chapter's myths or truths in Box 6.1. The answers and explanations are provided at the end of the chapter.

PREREQUISITES: ESTABLISHING A SOLID FOUNDATION

Early Intervention

Although the importance of engaging children in school and learning during the elementary school years was highlighted in Chapter 4, the evidence in support of early intervention programs for children from birth to school entrance (for example, kindergarten) in establishing a solid foundation and ultimately impacting rates of school completion deserves mention. Space does not permit a complete review of the long-term effects of early childhood intervention on educational achievement and subsequent graduation; however, several important points are highlighted. The reader is encouraged to consult the list of resources at the end of this chapter for further in-depth reading.

Research that focuses on early intervention prior to entering school is generally organized according to those programs that are geared for children age birth to 2 and those that target children 3 to 5 years old. Research shows that brain growth is greatest between the ages of zero to 3, and that there are critical periods within this age range for the development of some key language, motor, and sensory abilities. It is difficult to find longitudinal studies that clearly document the benefit of programs designated for infants and toddlers in relation to school completion. Certainly, identifying and addressing problems early, as well as fostering optimal conditions to provide opportunities for learning and growth during these early years, is desirable. However, providing early intervention during the preschool years (ages 3–5) is also valuable. Although the research on programs and interventions during the preschool years is more conclusive, many of the studies vary in terms of quality. Several longitudinal studies have been conducted that have incorporated random assignment and follow children at least as far as middle school (for example, Perry Preschool Project, Carolina Abcedarian Project, Milwaukee Project). Findings from these studies suggest positive benefits for children who participate in early intervention programs.

Specific goals of early intervention programs vary, but in general, short-term goals include providing a secure, stimulating environment that also addresses the needs for basic healthy development (such as nutritional needs). The long-term goal of early intervention is to positively impact outcomes that result in higher educational achievement, higher graduation rates, fewer arrests and involvement in criminal activity, and higher earnings. However, because tracking students longitudinally is difficult, more immediate goals, such as readiness to learn upon entrance to kindergarten or school performance in the early grades, are often measured. Of course, the hypothesis suggests that if students are more likely to be successful in school, they are more likely to have better long-term outcomes, including graduating with a diploma.

A review of research on programs implemented during the preschool years suggests these experiences can have beneficial effects on many of the protective factors associated with school completion. For example, outcomes include fewer referrals to special education, fewer retentions, higher grades, greater academic motivation and on-task behavior, lower incidence of absenteeism, lower incidence of pregnancy, drug abuse, and delinquency, and higher future aspirations. Outcomes are stronger for those programs that have certain characteristics in place (safe, clean, low staff-to-student ratio) and are characterized by a classroom process that is cognitively engaging and employs skillful and sensitive caregivers. While a clear causal relationship between participation in preschool programs and later success has not been clearly established, it is believed "that good early experiences can set in motion a chain of events that pervades the child's life through high school and beyond, increasing the quality of his/her life experiences along the way" (Cotton & Conklin, p. 6). An example of an early intervention program that yielded long-term effects is presented in Box 6.2.

Effective Schools

Effective schooling practices also help to lay the foundation for keeping students in school by creating the overall educational environment necessary for them to be successful. Similarly, a seedling that is planted in good soil, with enough water, and favorable weather conditions will be more likely to bloom as it matures. Just like the seedling, a school with effective practices in place increases the likelihood that students will be successful learners and have positive school experiences.

Although it is logical to assume these best practices will effectively increase the holding power of schools and subsequently the rate at which students complete

Box 6.2   Long-Term Effects of an Early Childhood Intervention

The Child-Parent Center (CPC) program is described as a center-based, preschool and early intervention program that offers family and educational support services. The program is based in Chicago and is operated through the school district with a focus on literacy development and parent involvement. The program is available to children ages 3–9. A longitudinal study followed the progress of CPC students over a period of 15 years. The majority of the students who participated in the longitudinal study were African American (93%) and were living below the poverty line (84%). The study examined the effects of CPC programs for each of the participants. Findings indicated students who attended CPC had greater levels of school readiness upon entering kindergarten or first grade, higher school achievement test scores, lower rates of juvenile arrest, and higher rates of school completion compared to those who did not participate in the program. Cost benefit analyses suggested the benefits to youth and society exceed the costs of the program, and results support the additional programming.

NOTE: For more information, see American Youth Policy Forum Brief. (2001). *The Long-Term Effects of an Early Childhood Intervention on Educational Achievement and Juvenile Arrest.* Retrieved September 28, 2004, from http://www.aypf.org/forumbriefs/2001/fb061801.htm

school successfully, we have few longitudinal studies that provide a direct empirical link establishing or isolating the effect of specific dimensions of effective schools on rates of graduation. Therefore, we cannot definitively state which pieces must be in place to yield the greatest impact on the numbers of students graduating with competence. However, we can identify many practices from research on effective schools that appear to be compatible with research-based practices that prevent students from dropping out.

One compilation of effective schooling research by the Northwest Regional Educational Laboratory (NWREL) divides these practices and characteristics into eight topic areas:

- *Leadership, Planning, and Learning Goals.* Practices and characteristics that address lifelong learning, preplanned curriculum, curriculum integration, work readiness skills, and educational technology
- *Management and Organization.* Practices and characteristics that address learning time, classroom routines, discipline, physical surroundings, and small-scale learning environments
- *Instruction and Instructional Improvement.* Practices and characteristics that address quality instruction, feedback to students, reteaching material, critical and creative thinking skills, and professional development
- *Interactions.* Practices and characteristics that address high expectations, incentives, recognition and rewards, and positive interactions with students
- *Equity.* Practices and characteristics that address additional learning time and instruction, social and academic resiliency, interactions among students of different socioeconomic and cultural backgrounds, and multicultural education
- *Special Programs.* Practices and characteristics that address preventing tobacco, alcohol, and drug use, providing activities for dropout-prone students, and connecting with community agencies

- *Assessment.* Practices and characteristics that address monitoring student progress and utilizing multiple methods of assessment
- *Parent and Community Involvement.* Practices and characteristics that address parent and community members involvement in children's learning and school governance, and policies that support parent and community involvement

Examples of specific practices in these topic areas that enhance student learning are listed in Table 6.1.

These practices are part of the educational underpinnings that serve a critical role in student success in school and learning. Even with these foundational building blocks in place, we believe there will continue to be students who struggle to complete school because they are placed at risk due to a variety of circumstances—many of them beyond their control. For these students, we have knowledge based on theory, research, and evidence-based dropout prevention programs that can help us to make informed decisions about what can be done to help keep them in school.

Table 6.1   Examples of Practices From Research on Effective Schools

- Teachers integrate workplace readiness skills into content-area instruction
- Administrators and teachers include workplace preparation among school goals
- Administrators and teachers establish and enforce clear, consistent discipline policies
- Administrators and teachers provide a pleasant physical environment for teaching and learning
- Administrators and teachers work to create and maintain small-scale learning environments
- Teachers provide clear and focused instruction
- Teachers review and reteach as necessary to help all students master learning material
- Administrators and other leaders continually strive to improve instructional effectiveness
- Teachers hold high expectations for student learning
- Teachers interact with students in positive, caring ways
- Teachers give high-needs students the extra time and instruction they need to succeed
- Teachers promote respect and empathy among students of different socioeconomic and cultural backgrounds
- School leaders and staff collaborate with community agencies to support families with urgent health and/or social service needs
- Teachers monitor student progress closely
- Teachers involve parents and community members in supporting children's learning

NOTE: This list is not meant to be comprehensive, but includes a sample of practices only. For more information, the reader is encouraged to see the associated reference.

SOURCE: Adapted from Cotton, K. (1999). *Research you can use to improve results.* Portland, OR: Northwest Regional Educational Laboratory. Used with permission.

TYPES AND EXAMPLES OF INTERVENTIONS DESIGNED TO ADDRESS DROPOUT

Several reviews of effective dropout prevention programs and strategies suggest there is more than one way to effectively increase graduation rates. The programs and strategies vary widely in their focus. For example, some of the interventions are designed to influence a student's academic success through direct intervention such as tutoring. Others focus on changing the structure of the school environment to enhance student and staff relationships and help students develop a stronger sense of belonging. Still others focus on increasing the connections between home and school and strengthening parent involvement to build student engagement in school and learning.

There Is More Than One (Right) Way of Doing Things

Although the number of research studies on effective interventions published in professional journals is limited, the strategies that are used to keep students in school vary widely. Forty-five studies focused on preventing dropout that were published in professional journals from 1980 to 2001 included interventions that could be organized into five categories:

- *Personal Affective.* These interventions focused on conveying the importance of staying in school and helped students to cope with challenging personal problems, and improve relationships, self-confidence, and problem-solving skills. Strategies included regularly scheduled classroom-based discussion (addressing motivation, relevance of school, career goals), counseling sessions, support groups, an interpersonal relations class, and other specialized curriculum (teaching positive school behavior, responsibility, asking for help).
- *Academic.* These interventions focused on improving students' academic performance and included providing special academic courses, tutoring, implementing team meetings to review student progress, and providing instruction on study skills.
- *Family Outreach.* These strategies were designed to increase communication between home and school, parent involvement in school and parenting skills. Examples included home visits, inviting parents to be part of school teams, offering parent support groups, and providing feedback to parents on student progress more frequently.
- *School Structure.* These interventions changed the school environment to build more caring and personalized relationships, individual attention, and personalized programming. Examples included implementing a school within a school, redefining the role of the homeroom teacher, reducing class sizes, modifying block schedules, and creating an alternative school.
- *Work Related.* Work-related strategies included offering vocational training, volunteer opportunities, and service learning programs.

Seventy-one percent of the interventions in the 45 studies addressed students' personal or emotional experiences. Nearly one-half of the studies were designed to enhance academic performance and learning skills. Many of the interventions that

Box 6.3 Multiple Goals and Strategies. The Ninth Grade Dropout Prevention Program

The *Ninth Grade Dropout Prevention Program* was originally implemented in six high schools in Florida. Each school was responsible for designing its own intervention plan to decrease dropout by meeting specific goals, which included addressing students' academic needs, creating a caring atmosphere, and providing relevant and challenging curriculum. To address academic performance, strategies included tutoring (for example, homework hotline, teacher assistance, peer tutoring), teaming/cooperative planning (for example, establishing ninth grade teams, utilizing paraprofessionals to assist teams), and staff development (for example, teacher in-service on dropout research). Each school incorporated an orientation component for incoming freshmen that included providing information to students during registration, offering a buddy system, and holding class meetings. Parents received information about the program via letters, telephone calls, and newsletters. Attendance was also addressed by identifying students who were frequently absent, offering support services (social worker), and providing awards for good attendance. *The Ninth Grade Prevention Program* is a good example of an intervention model that utilized a variety of strategies to address student needs and goals of the program. (For more information, see Pearson & Banerji, 1993.)

were reviewed included strategies that fell in multiple categories. An example of a program that included multiple goals and strategies is provided in Box 6.3.

Examples of Effective Interventions

There are several examples of interventions that have evidence of effectiveness and are published in the research literature. Each is intended to meet a specific need, but the ultimate goal is to increase school completion. All of the interventions work to keep students engaged in school. Box 6.4 lists several sources that can be consulted to identify and find more information about programs that have been used to prevent dropout.

We highlight five examples here that reflect different approaches to addressing dropout. We are giving you just a snapshot of these interventions here. We encourage you to read the references listed for more information on the examples that interest you (see Further Reading at the end of the chapter).

- *Check & Connect.* A model designed to engage students in school and learning via a mentor or monitor who establishes a long-term relationship and maintains regular contact with the student, family, and teachers. Risk factors are systematically monitored and interventions tailored to meet individual student needs, such as increased communication with parents, tutoring, and problem solving. For more information, see Sinclair, Christenson, and Thurlow (2005).
- *Support Center for Adolescent Mothers.* The family support center was developed to provide social and educational supports to teen mothers in order to prevent repeat pregnancy and school dropout. Four key components of the

---

Box 6.4   Resources That Identify and Describe Programs to Prevent Dropout

These resources provide listings and descriptions of programs that have been used to address the problem of dropout. See them for more information about specific programs.

Fashola, O. S., & Slavin, R. E. (1998). Effective dropout prevention and college attendance programs for students placed at risk. *Journal of Education for Students Placed at Risk, 3*(2), 159–183.

Hayward, B. J., & Tallmadge, G. K. (1995). *Strategies for keeping kids in school: Evaluation of dropout prevention and reentry projects in vocational education.* (U.S. Department of Education, final report). Washington, DC: U.S. Government Printing Office.

Lehr, C. A., Johnson, D. R., Bremer, C. D., Cosio, A., & Thompson, M. (2003). *Increasing rates of school completion: Moving from policy and research to practice. NCSET Essential Tools.* University of Minnesota: Institute on Community Integration, National Center on Secondary Education and Transition.

Prevatt, F., & Kelly, F. D. (2003). Dropping out of school: A review of intervention programs. *Journal of School Psychology, 41,* 377–395.

Shargel, F. P., & Smink, J. (2001). *Strategies to help solve our school dropout problem.* Larchmont, NY: Eye on Education.

---

model include establishing early contact with the mothers, involving families, implementing parenting education groups, and involving the community. For more information, see Solomon and Liefeld (1998).

- *School Transitional Environment Project.* The goal of this prevention program is to enhance healthy school adjustment during school transitions by restructuring the environmental characteristics of school settings. For example, students take primary academics with a cohort of students, classrooms are arranged in close proximity, and homeroom teachers serve as counselors and link between students, families, and schools. For more information, see Felner and colleagues (1993).

- *Teen Outreach Program.* This program was designed to prevent teen pregnancy and school dropout for both males and females by having students volunteer in their communities and participate in classroom-based discussions on a weekly basis for one school year. Key elements include learning life skills, discussing social and emotional issues, and participating in volunteer service opportunities in the community. For more information, see Allen, Philliber, and Hoggson (1990).

- *Personal Growth Class.* The semester-long personal growth classes are designed to prevent drug abuse and school dropout among high school students identified as high risk for school failure. The classes use an intensive school-based social network prevention approach. Key elements include experiential learning, study skills training, peer tutoring, and training in decision making provided by peers and teachers. For more information, see Eggert, Seyl, and Nicholas (1990).

LINKING THE INTERVENTION TO IDENTIFIED NEEDS

Using an intervention that is directly linked to the identified needs of the students, the school, or the district is critically important. It makes little sense to implement an intervention that is designed to increase regular attendance when the overall attendance rate is high. On the other hand, if it is clear that many of the students who are dropping out of school are single teenage mothers who are pregnant or parenting, it makes sense to design or select a program that will provide education and support for the mothers and their children so that they can attend and finish school.

You have been gathering information and identifying needs of your students at the school or district level. You have information about the numbers of students who are dropping out, reasons why students are dropping out, and you have identified factors that are placing students at risk as well as those that keep kids in school. This knowledge can help to guide the design or selection of interventions to address identified needs. Remember, just because a program was effective in one setting does not mean that the program will be effective in your setting. The needs of your students must be carefully considered and an intervention aligned that will address the needs and goals. To illustrate, simplified examples of student needs and possible types of interventions are listed in Table 6.2.

Table 6.2   Aligning Interventions With Identified Needs

Identified Need or Problem	Possible Intervention
Students are failing classes and not coming to school due to significant drug and alcohol abuse	Provide intensive school-based chemical dependency counseling and skill-building program using a preventive social networking approach
High numbers of students are dropping out of school due to pregnancy and parenting	Offer educational sessions on life skills and competence enhancement as well as on-site day care and a support center for adolescent parents
Students are dropping out of school because they are working at jobs and see little relevance of a diploma for later job options	Link students with mentors from local businesses and provide service learning opportunities to explore career options
Students are failing classes due to lack of prerequisite language and academic skills	Provide intensive early intervention programs focused on early literacy skills for children from immigrant families
Students are dropping out of a large high school due to feelings of alienation and lack of belonging	Implement school climate evaluation and reform based on input from students, staff, and parents

LEVELS OF INTERVENTION

As you can see, interventions can be implemented at multiple levels and vary in complexity and comprehensiveness. Figure 6.1 shows three levels of interventions that are

Figure 6.1   Indicated, Selected, and Universal Interventions

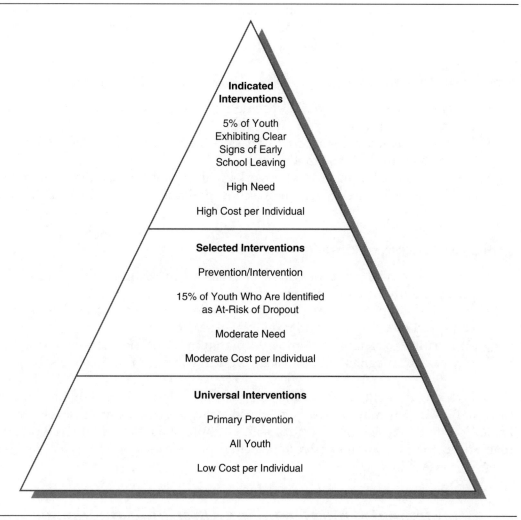

Indicated Interventions

5% of Youth Exhibiting Clear Signs of Early School Leaving

High Need

High Cost per Individual

Selected Interventions

Prevention/Intervention

15% of Youth Who Are Identified as At-Risk of Dropout

Moderate Need

Moderate Cost per Individual

Universal Interventions

Primary Prevention

All Youth

Low Cost per Individual

SOURCE: The path to school failure, delinquency, and violence: Causal factors and some potential solutions. By H. M. Walker & J. R. Sprague (1999). *Intervention in School and Clinic, 35,* 67–73. Copyright 1999 by PRO-ED, Inc. Adapted with permission.

commonly described in the research literature. In general, *universal* interventions are designed for all students and are usually implemented at the school or classroom level. *Selected* interventions are designed to address the needs of students who have been identified as at risk. *Indicated* interventions are typically geared for a small percentage of students who are at high risk and are showing clear signs of leaving school early.

Researchers at the University of Oregon conducted a review of interventions designed to prevent dropout and categorized them according to whether they were universal, selected, or indicated interventions. Examples of each type of intervention include:

Universal Interventions

- Student advisory programs that monitor academic and social development of middle or high school students
- Efforts to engage students in extracurricular activities (especially those with a vocational or athletic focus)

- School-to-work programs that foster success in school through linkages to employers and educational opportunities
- Systemic positive discipline programs that work to build welcoming school environments, favorable school climate, and caring relationships

Selected Interventions

- Programs that work to build specific skills such as problem solving, anger control, or interpersonal communication
- Providing additional support to an identified group of students through a "school within a school" model
- Providing an adult mentor who works with students and families on a long-term basis to foster engagement in school and deliver the message that school is important

Indicated Interventions

- Specific behavior plans or contracts designed to address individual student needs and produce positive outcomes
- Intensive wrap-around services that provide an individualized package of coordinated community and school-level services
- Alternative programs that provide parenting education classes and on-site day care for pregnant and parenting youth who have not finished school

Addressing student needs at all levels is most desirable, although you need to recognize that it may not be possible to provide services at all levels. Miami Dade County Public Schools, Florida, is an example of a district that has worked to plan and deliver a comprehensive model that provides service across all levels of intervention (see Box 6.5).

Implementation Scenario: Clarifying the Focus: Prevention and Intervention Programs (January)

At this point, some of the committee members were getting anxious to move forward and put a program in place to address the needs that had been identified. The committee members had gathered lots of useful information, but they still were not sure what to do about it! It was decided that the next phase of work needed to focus on identifying a list of programs that were already in place with goals linked to preventing dropout and promoting student engagement in school and learning. Initially, committee members brainstormed a list of programs. They generated a list of 10 programs, such as a program funded by Title I to help struggling readers in first and second grade, an after-school help group provided at the middle school level, a ninth grade orientation program to assist with transition to high school, and a collaborative effort with the community counseling agency to work with students who were chemically dependent. Individuals from these programs were invited to share information with the district committee, especially in relation to impact on school completion. This meeting generated an awareness of the importance of clearly documenting outcomes for students who were involved in these programs and in some cases resulted in identifying indicators of impact related to engagement

> **Box 6.5**   A Comprehensive System to Address Dropout—Miami Dade
> Public Schools
>
> ___
>
> Miami Dade County Public Schools offers several programs at a variety of levels designed
> to increase graduation rates. Through early intervention, counseling, mentoring, and
> other strategies, students are provided assistance to succeed in school. A sample of some
> of the programs that are offered are listed below.
>
> *Building Early Language and Literacy.* The program is offered in pre-kindergarten early
> intervention sites to build the foundational skills for good readers through the develop-
> ment of oral language, vocabulary and concepts, early comprehension, phonological
> awareness/pre-phonemic skills.
>
> *Standards-Based Student Career Development Program.* Student services staff assist
> students in the use of Career Planning Portfolios to enhance the process of career devel-
> opment and in assisting students with post secondary planning. Students are exposed to
> career fairs, job shadowing, mentoring, career interest inventories, portfolio develop-
> ment, and other career related programs.
>
> *Take Stock in Children.* This program provides at-risk students who meet specific criteria
> (e.g., income guidelines, grades) with a mentor. Students who commit to and maintain
> good grades, stay drug-free and crime-free receive a full tuition scholarship to college or
> a vocational/technical school.
>
> *Teenage Parent Program (TAP).* This program provides students who are teenage parents
> with the services to assist them in completing their education while providing child care,
> transportation, health services, social service and counseling.
>
> SOURCE: Miami-Dade County Public Schools Programs That Impact the Graduation and Dropout
> Rates (2003). Adapted with permission from Miami Dade County Public Schools Florida.

and school completion (for example, measuring improvement in school attendance for students receiving counseling for chemical dependency). Careful attention was also given to linking information gathered from previous meetings about reasons or risk factors contributing to the problem of dropout to an identified need—and determining how the programs in place met that need.

Although this meeting suggested that the district had programs in place to assist students at risk of dropout, some gaps were also identified. For example, options for students who left school and wanted to return were limited. Lack of recovery programs were especially limited in light of the high number of students who became pregnant in high school and left school while parenting. The only options in place included returning to high school or enrolling in a GED program. Gathering information on existing programs provided a much more comprehensive picture and helped to clarify useful programs that were already in place as well as areas that needed to be addressed.

SUMMARY

In this chapter we identified several types of interventions and provided examples of interventions that have shown evidence of effectiveness in research studies.

Knowledge of the variety of interventions that have been tried and that have been successful suggests that there is not one best strategy or program to use. One of the keys to success is linking the intervention directly to the need that must be addressed. Clear identification of the problem also assists in choosing the level at which the intervention should be implemented—universal, selected, or indicated. In most cases, it makes sense to have a comprehensive set of programs or strategies that can provide a preventative approach geared for all students as well as programs that target students who are at risk and at high risk for drop out.

Now check your knowledge of the Myth or Truth? statements from the beginning of the chapter (see Box 6.6 for answers). Check your understanding against the explanations.

Box 6.6   Myth or Truth? Answers

1. **Myth.** The most effective strategy for addressing the problem of dropout has been clearly identified, is well researched, and has been replicated in multiple settings. *Explanation:* Many programs have been studied and some are effective, but there is not one program that is clearly the best. (See page 113.)

2. **Truth.** Most interventions that have been systematically reviewed use multiple strategies to address the problem of dropout. *Explanation:* Most interventions use multiple strategies that fall into one of five categories: personal affective, academic, family outreach, school structure and work related. (See page 113.)

3. **Myth.** Interventions that include a family outreach component are the most commonly used means of addressing dropout. *Explanation:* In a review of dropout interventions, the most commonly used strategies were those that addressed personal affective needs or academic performance. (See page 113.)

4. **Truth.** Universal interventions are a useful preventive approach for promoting school completion and typically target a large percentage of students. *Explanation:* Universal interventions are prevention oriented, operate at a systemic level and are typically geared for all students. (See page 117.)

5. **Myth.** It is nearly impossible to provide interventions to decrease dropout across all three levels (universal, selected and indicated). *Explanation:* Comprehensive dropout prevention program at the district level exist and include interventions that are preventive as well as those that are targeted for students at risk and those at high risk of leaving school early. (See page 118.)

REFLECTION QUESTIONS

1. Think about the types and examples of interventions described in this chapter. How are they similar to programs or strategies that are being implemented in your setting? How are they different?

2. Chapter 4 described dropping out as a process and emphasized the importance of engaging students early, during critical transition times, and recovering students who left school. Discuss the types of interventions that might be used to address these specific situations.

3. Consider the three levels of intervention—universal, selected, and indicated. What are the strengths and challenges of implementing programs to promote school completion and prevent dropout for each level?

FURTHER READING

American Youth Policy Forum Brief. (2001). *The long-term effects of an early childhood intervention on educational achievement and juvenile arrest.* Retrieved September 28, 2004, from http://www.aypf.org/forumbriefs/2001/fb061801.htm

Allen, J. P., Philliber, S., & Hoggson, N. (1990). School-based prevention of teen-age pregnancy and school dropout: Process evaluation on the national replication of the teen outreach program. *American Journal of Community Psychology, 18,* 505–524.

Cotton, K. (1999). *Research you can use to improve results.* Portland, OR: Northwest Regional Educational Laboratory.

Cotton, K., & Conklin, N. F. (2001). Research on early childhood education. *School Improvement Research Series* (Topical Synthesis #3). Portland, OR: Northwest Regional Educational Laboratory.

Dynarski, M., & Gleason, P. (2002). How can we help? What we have learned from federal dropout prevention programs. *Journal of Education for Students Placed at Risk, 7*(1), 43–69.

Eggert, L. L., Seyl, C. D., & Nicholas, L. J. (1990). Effects of a school-based prevention program for potential high school dropouts and drug abusers. *International Journal of the Addictions, 25*(7), 773–801.

Fashola, O. S., & Slavin, R. E. (1998). Effective dropout prevention and college attendance programs for students placed at risk. *Journal of Education for Students Placed at Risk, 3*(2), 159–183.

Felner, R. D., Brand, S., Adan, A. M., Mulhall, P. F., Flowers, N., Sartain, B., & DuBois, D. L. (1993). Restructuring the ecology of the school as an approach to prevention during school transitions: Longitudinal follow-ups and extensions for the School Transitional Environment Project (STEP). *Prevention in Human Services, 10*(2), 103–136.

Hayward, B. J., & Tallmadge, G. K. (1995). *Strategies for keeping kids in school: Evaluation of dropout prevention and reentry projects in vocational education* (U.S. Department of Education, final report). Washington, DC: U.S. Government Printing Office.

Lehr, C. A. (2004). Increasing school completion: Learning from research-based practices that work. *Research to Practice Brief, 3*(3). University of Minnesota: Institute on Community Integration, National Center on Secondary Education and Transition.

Lehr, C. A., Hansen, A., Sinclair, M. F., & Christenson, S. L. (2003). Moving beyond dropout prevention to school completion: An integrative review of data-based interventions. *School Psychology Review, 32*(3), 342–364.

Lehr, C. A., Johnson, D., Bremer, C. D., Cosio, A., & Thompson, M. (2003). *Increasing rates of school completion: Moving from policy and research to practice. NCSET Essential Tools.* University of Minnesota: Institute on Community Integration, National Center on Secondary Education and Transition.

Martin, E. J., Tobin, T. J, & Sugai, G. M. (2002). Current information on dropout prevention: Ideas from practitioners and the literature. *Preventing School Failure, 47*(1), 10–17.

Pearson, L. C., & Banerji, M. (1993). Effects of a ninth-grade dropout prevention program on student academic achievement, school attendance, and dropout rate. *Journal of Experimental Education, 61*(3), 247–256.

Prevatt, F., & Kelly, F. D. (2003). Dropping out of school: A review of intervention programs. *Journal of School Psychology, 41,* 377–395.

Shonkoff, J. P., & Meisels, S. J. (2000). *Handbook of early childhood intervention* (2nd ed.). New York: Cambridge University Press.

Sinclair, M. F., Christenson, S. L., & Thurlow, M. L. (2005). Promoting school completion of urban secondary youth with emotional or behavioral disabilities. *Exceptional Children,* (4).

Solomon, R., & Liefeld, C. P. (1998). Effectiveness of a family support center approach to adolescent mothers: Repeat pregnancy and school drop-out rates. *Family Relations: Interdisciplinary Journal of Applied Family Studies, 47,* 139–144.

Walker, H. M., & Sprague, J. R. (1999). The path to school failure, delinquency, and violence: Causal factors and some potential solutions. *Intervention in School and Clinic, 35*(2), 67–73.

TAKING ACTION

This section is for those of you who are ready to begin doing something to decrease the number of students dropping out of school. But, before interventions can be selected or designed to address dropout and school completion in your setting, you need to dig deeper and determine answers to basic questions to inform decision making. Action Tools are provided in this section.

At this point, it will be helpful to identify existing programs in your setting that are specifically designed to engage students and prevent dropout. For example, what early intervention programs are in place, and are students followed longitudinally to determine outcomes? Programs that engage students in preschool or the early grades and provide necessary prerequisite skills for school success are critical preventive measures. Students and families who are receiving assistance in addressing difficulties that emerge early on are more likely to have success in school and stay to completion. A sample form that can be used to compile and review this information is included in this section. You may also want to document educational options that are available to students who are not successful in conventional schools, and identify programs already in place that engage students including recovery programs, extracurricular options, and programs to facilitate smooth transitions between schools.

Depending on your circumstances, there are a number of directions you can go from here. To determine what your next move should be, we recommend that you read through the questions in the left-hand column of the Guide to Action Tools, identify your most immediate needs, and then use the Action Tool listed in the right-hand column to gather the information you need. It is important to remember that the Action Tools are sample forms that are provided to assist you in gathering and organizing data that will help you to make informed decisions about how to address dropout in your setting. The tools can be reproduced; however, they may need to be modified to meet the needs of your school or district. Be sure to check whether there are district or school policies or procedures that must be followed before proceeding with the activities you plan to carry out.

GUIDE TO ACTION TOOLS

What Do You Need to Know or Do?	Action Tool
Identify programs that are in place to address school completion	Action Tool 6.1: *Individual Program Description Form*
Compare programs that are in place to address school completion	Action Tool 6.2: *Comparing Programs Mapping Tool*
Identify extracurricular activities that are in place to engage students	Action Tool 6.3: *Extracurricular Options Mapping Form*

ACTION TOOL 6.1 INDIVIDUAL PROGRAM DESCRIPTION FORM

Objectives: To examine individual programs that are being used to help students complete school

Instructions:

1. List existing programs to examine. These might include existing *early intervention programs* that follow students through school to determine program impact on graduation, *programs that facilitate successful critical transitions* (for example, middle school to high school), *existing programs that prevent dropout for students in Grades 6–12* by engaging students in learning, *alternative educational options* for students who are not succeeding in conventional schools, or *programs that are designed to recover youth who have left* school.

2. Identify sources that can be used to provide information about each program. For example, sources might include an existing program description, the director or coordinator of a program, or a technical report.

3. Using one Action Tool for each program, record information for each of the categories provided.

Follow-Up:

1. Review the information gathered and recorded. Determine strengths for each program.

2. Discuss what needs (in relation to school completion) are being met through these programs.

School/District _____

ACTION TOOL 6.1 INDIVIDUAL PROGRAM DESCRIPTION FORM

Name of Program/Contact Person	
Year Started	
Funding (Amount and source)	
Target Audience (Multiple audiences may be identified)	
Grades/Ages Served	
Purpose/Objectives/Focus (e.g., literacy, social skills, attendance)	
When Services Are Provided	
Where Services Are Provided (Location)	
Collaborating Agencies	
Family Involvement Component (Describe)	
Outcomes (Record available data)	
Are students followed longitudinally to determine enrollment status?	

ACTION TOOL 6.2   COMPARING PROGRAMS MAPPING TOOL

Objectives: To compare programs in order to identify strengths, overlap, and gaps in existing programming that is being used to help students complete school

Instructions:

1. List existing programs that are in place to help students complete school. You may want to refer to programs identified and described using Action Tool 6.1: Individual Program Description Form.

2. Gather information and place an X in the appropriate categories listed on the mapping tool.

Follow-Up:

1. Review the information gathered and recorded. Determine strengths, overlap, and gaps.

2. Develop a Summary Statement and discuss action steps you might take to address identified areas of need.

School/District _____

ACTION TOOL 6.2   COMPARING PROGRAMS MAPPING TOOL

Program Title and Description (Multiple forms may be required)	Early Intervention Program	Programs to Help With Transition	Dropout Prevention in Middle Schools	Dropout Prevention in High Schools	Alternative Education Options	Recovery Programs
Program A						
Program B						
Program C						
Program D						
Program E						
Summary Statement:						

ACTION TOOL 6.3   EXTRACURRICULAR OPTIONS MAPPING FORM

Objective: To identify available extracurricular activities and the extent of student involvement

Materials: Student Handbook and other sources of information that identify extracurricular programs

Instructions:

1. Review documents and list extracurricular options that are available to students. These may include sports (basketball, hockey, softball, baseball, track); theater; clubs (chess, computer, skiing); music (jazz band, concert band, marching band); student council; school yearbook; honors; community service projects.

2. Gather program information and data. If possible, disaggregate the information by subgroups (gender, ethnicity, disability).

3. Record information on the Action Tool.

Follow-Up:

1. Review the information gathered and recorded. Determine strengths and gaps.

2. Discuss whether you are reaching all students. What strategies are you using to engage those students who are not participating? Who is in charge of inviting students to be a part of these extracurricular groups?

3. Develop a Summary Statement. Determine whether needs are being addressed and discuss action steps to address identified needs.

School/District _____

ACTION TOOL 6.3   EXTRACURRICULAR OPTIONS MAPPING FORM

Activity	Number of Students Participating Total Number of Students in School	(If possible disaggregate by subgroups)	How Students Percentage of Total School Population	Participate (Selective, open to all, referred)

Summary Statement:

7

Putting the Pieces Together

TOPICS

- Organizing Your Data
- Identifying and Prioritizing Needs
- Creating a Progress Report
- Revising Your Communication Plan

IN THIS CHAPTER, YOU WILL . . .

- Learn about a strategy for organizing data
- Consider criteria for prioritizing needs
- Explore the possibility of creating a report to summarize your work
- Think about key messages for stakeholder groups and how to communicate with them

We believe you need to have a fundamental understanding of the dropout process in order to develop effective programs—programs that result in higher rates of school completion. In Chapters 3 through 6, research-based information helped you understand:

- Graduation and dropout statistics and reasons for their variability, dropout rates for student subgroups, terminology, and procedures for calculating rates (Chapter 3)

Box 7.1   Myth or Truth? Do You Know?

Read each statement following and decide whether it is a myth or the truth.

1. Once you have identified your findings, you need to analyze them to determine the root causes of the problems.

2. Prioritizing your needs based on specific criteria will help you to use your resources more effectively.

3. Creating a report of your progress at this point in the process can serve many purposes.

4. It is important to think carefully about the type and amount of information you should share with various stakeholder groups.

5. If the information you have collected presents a less than positive picture of your school, it should not be reported to the public.

- Reasons why students drop out of school and why they stay in, along with an explanation of dropping out as a process of disengagement (Chapter 4)
- Status and alterable factors that place students at risk of dropping out of school and the importance of engaging students in school (Chapter 5), and
- Examples of effective interventions used to prevent dropout and an explanation of levels of implementation (Chapter 6)

At the end of each chapter, Reflection Questions prompted you to consider, think about, and discuss the chapter's topics with others. A section called "Taking Action" was included in each chapter for those readers who want to gather additional information relevant to their setting and use it for further planning.

If you have been gathering additional information, this chapter will help you organize and analyze that information. Further, it will help you identify and prioritize your needs, create a summary of your work, and revise your communication plan.

Before you begin, review the Myth or Truth? statements in Box 7.1. Be prepared to check your answers at the end of the chapter.

ORGANIZING YOUR DATA

Throughout the information-gathering process, the Action Tools you used probably depended on your current situation. If you used all the Action Tools presented in the previous chapters, you have a lot of information. Even if you just used a few of them, what you have collected needs to be organized and analyzed.

To make sense of everything you have collected so far, start by listing all the Action Tools you used. Then write a short description of the steps you took when you used them and a summary of the results (see Table 7.1).

While you might think that writing down your findings means you have identified the need, you have not. You still need to think about why you might

Table 7.1   Example of Key Findings Summary

Name of Action Tool	Description of Action Taken and Sources of Data	Key Findings
Action Tool 4.2: *Student Interview Guide*	The action team identified 30 students who had dropped out and then returned to school. Because they were all under the age of 18, we obtained written permission from their parents to conduct the interview, and we also had the students give their written consent as well. All 30 students agreed to be interviewed, and the interviews took place over a two-month period. The interviews were conducted by four members of the action team who had received training from the university on conducting interviews. Audiotapes were made of each interview. The action team worked with the university to analyze the results of the interviews.	• When asked, "At what grade did you drop out of school?" 98% of students interviewed said they dropped out for the first time in the ninth grade. • When asked, "Why did you decide to drop out?" 85% of the students interviewed reported that one of the reasons was related to poor academic performance, failing grades, or failing courses. • When asked, "How did the school try to help with your academic problems?" 90% of the students interviewed said that they did not receive any additional academic help from the school.
Action Tool 4.3: *Student Checklist*	The action team located the names and addresses of 200 students who had dropped out in the past five years and sent them surveys. 100 individuals returned their surveys. We counted the number of responses for each response and identified the five most common reasons for dropping out according to the individuals we surveyed.	The five most common reasons given for dropping out of school: • Dislike of school or school environment • Expulsion from school • Poor grades/failing grades • Job opportunity • Pregnancy
Action Tool 5.3: *Board Policy Analysis Form*	The action team reviewed existing board policies on: Attendance; Truancy; Discipline; Suspension; Grading; Retention; and Failing Grades. We assigned a score for each policy based on its impact on school completion with a "1" being a negative impact; "3" being neutral; and "5" a positive impact.	Board policies perceived to have a negative impact (scored 1 or 2): *Policy A* imposes out-of-school suspension for minor infractions of school rules. *Policy B* stipulates that students who are truant be placed in out-of-school suspension. *Policy C* requires teachers to lower grades for truancy.

have obtained the results that you did. We recommend that you apply the Five Why process you learned in Chapter 4 to determine the root cause of the problem. Building in this step before settling on what appears to be the obvious—but possibly inaccurate—statement of need will ensure that your conclusions are based on the real problem, not the symptoms.

IDENTIFYING AND PRIORITIZING NEEDS

Once you have identified your statements of need, you may find that the list of problem areas in your school is a long one. If that is the case, you may need to think about prioritizing your list. One way to do that is to think about the various criteria you would like to use to guide you in the priority-setting process. These criteria might include the importance of the problem, the feasibility of solving it, and the amount of time and money solving it will take. Once you have identified the criteria, you can take each of your identified needs, lay it against the criteria to see how it fares, and then assign it a priority.

For example, maybe one of your identified needs is the high number of students dropping out in Grade 9 because they lack the reading skills needed to be successful in their courses. You may decide that this need is very important, that it is something that is possible for you to solve, but that it might require a large investment in professional development for teachers or the hiring of reading specialists for the middle school. Even though the cost of solving that problem is high, you may decide that it is a top priority, and that it needs to go to the top of the list. You may find that ther needs you identify, while important, will be difficult to solve and require more funds than you have available. For example, you might find that you have students who could best be served in an alternative setting, but the district does not have the resources to support establishing a school for these students. Even though the need is great, this issue might have to go to the bottom of your list. One way to prioritize needs is shown in Table 7.2.

The way you go about prioritizing needs is not the issue. What is important is that you come up with a defensible way to select the needs that will be addressed

Table 7.2   Example of a Prioritization Matrix

Priority	Statements of Need	Importance *(5 = High Importance)*	Feasibility *(5 = High Feasibility)*	Cost *(5 = Low Cost)*	Total Score
2	Ninth grade students lack basic reading skills	5	5	2	12
1	School board policies contain language that has a negative impact on school completion	5	5	5	15
4	A significant proportion of families of students provide limited support for learning	4	1	1	6
3	The community has limited chemical dependency supports available to assist students	5	2	1	8

first. You must do this, because you do not have the time or money to do everything at the same time.

CREATING A PROGRESS REPORT

Although you have all the information you need to select a dropout prevention program, this is a good time to create a report of your process. Putting everything together in one document ensures that your hard work is not lost. It also creates a context for the needs you identified and provides a rationale for the decisions you make about how to address those needs.

Your progress report requires little more than bringing forward your answers to the questions that were raised, the results of the Action Tools that you used, and the conclusions you reached, and placing them in one report. Doing this is especially important if you are part of an action team working as part of a broader school improvement process. If this is the case, the report can serve as a formal record of your process, a means of communicating with your audiences, a justification for your future decisions, and a baseline against which progress can be measured.

REVISING YOUR COMMUNICATION PLAN

Before you started collecting information, we suggested that you develop a plan to manage the communication of information. Since a lot has probably changed since you started your data collection process, this is a good time to revisit your existing communication plan and revise it. If you did not create a communication plan before, think about creating one now. Soon you will be selecting and implementing an intervention based on the needs of your students. It is important for people in the school and community to understand how you identified the challenges and how you arrived at the solutions for addressing those challenges.

The process for updating your communication plan is the same as the one you used to create the first one. Think about the key messages you want to share, determine who needs to hear which messages, and then identify a tool appropriate to the audience for delivering the messages. For example, through your data collection efforts you may have uncovered the fact that most of your students are dropping out in the ninth grade due to low reading skills and the inability to keep up with their coursework. Now you think that your next step is either to find an existing, research-based adolescent literacy program appropriate for middle-level students or to design one of your own. These are important pieces of information that stakeholders need to hear about in some form or other. Now is the time to think carefully about matching up messages, audiences, and communication vehicles.

Teachers and other school personnel will be interested in the results of the information-gathering process, so an e-mail update or memo detailing your findings is a good idea. For parents, an article in a newsletter or a posting on your school Web site providing a short update of what has been happening is a good communication option. If your plans involve the allocation of resources, talking to the school board about what you learned will help that group to begin thinking about the resources that may be needed in the future. All in all, a steady stream of accurate and appropriate information to all stakeholder groups is good practice at this point.

A word of caution may be in order here. If your school does not have a history of routinely gathering data and sharing it with the public, you might be reluctant to share what might be perceived as bad news. If this is your situation, you will want to think carefully about how to proceed as you share your findings with others. One way to prepare the public for this type of information is by first writing some general articles on the importance of a data-driven decision-making process. For example, you could write an article for the school newsletter or the local paper about why it is important to reveal, not conceal, data. In that article, you could emphasize the importance of using information to improve practice, not place blame, and provide examples from schools like yours, where collecting, sharing, and acting on data produced positive results for students. After creating a positive climate around the use of data, releasing the results of your self-study on dropout should fall on more receptive ears. An example of how the Houston Independent School District shared information with the public on its dropout problem through an "op-ed" piece in the Houston *Chronicle* is contained in Box 7.2.

Implementation Scenario: Putting the Pieces Together (February)

Meetings that were held at this stage of the process proved to be especially helpful, as the information that had been collected over the past few months was organized in a way that really helped to inform the next steps. First, the committee summarized key findings based on the information gathered up to this point. For example, the committee summarized findings (1) about the numbers and subgroups of students who were dropping out of school; (2) reasons for dropout and identification of when students were dropping out of school; (3) status and alterable variables placing student populations at risk; and (4) existing programs already in place. From here, the committee members began to have a clearer idea of the needs specific to the population of students being served in their district. The elementary, middle, and high school teams also mirrored this process for their respective schools. Quite a list of needs was identified, and so the committee decided to prioritize the needs and determine whether they were a high priority, whether the need was feasible to address, and what was the estimated cost of addressing the problem. Just to give you an idea, the highest priority identified at the district is briefly summarized here:

- *District Level.* Review of the data collected on an annual basis over the past three years showed the highest proportion of students who dropped out of school did so in ninth grade. Further investigation showed disproportionate representation of students from Latino families. Additional data gathered through student and parent interviews, discussion with counselors, and community members indicated several factors that were pushing and pulling students out of school. A liaison fluent in both Spanish and English was employed to assist in talking with parents who did not speak English. Parents were very supportive of their students attending school and getting a diploma; however, many of the parents worked long hours at the local packing plant, had recently migrated to the community, and did not feel particularly connected to the school community. Students also expressed an interest in

Box 7.2   HISD Accepts Challenge of Stemming Dropouts

The 2001–2002 school year has ended, and the Houston Independent School District succeeded in staying the course of academic achievement for all students and remains a leader in education reform. Texas Assessment of Academic Skills, or TAAS, scores were up across the board this year, the achievement gap between minority and nonminority students continues to narrow, and nearly 7,500 students graduated from HISD schools just weeks ago. However, there is still work to be done, especially in the area of graduation rates and combating the dropout problem. As school systems nationwide struggle to tackle this problem, HISD's Board of Education and the administration intend to take on the challenge and succeed.

Students leave school for many reasons, and that is the crux of the problem nationwide. There is no agreed-upon definition of the term dropout and no consistent data collection on dropouts. As a result, a state and/or nationwide tracking system and a consistently applied dropout rate become problematic. That makes it difficult for school districts to develop meaningful instructional programs specifically for students who are at risk of dropping out of the educational process entirely.

HISD has two different dropout rates, both of which are calculated by the state. One rate (15.3 percent in 2000) is the percentage of ninth-graders who dropped out and did not return at the end of four years. The other rate (3.2 percent in 2000) measures the number of students in grades seven through 12 who dropped out within a single year. Both calculations provide useful information, but they are complicated and subject to continuing debate.

Despite the complexities of student dropout identification and tracking, HISD has taken action to keep students in school. We raised promotion standards to eliminate social promotion, and we eliminated TAAS exemptions and developed a consistent districtwide curriculum that is aligned with the state's educational requirements. We require that students read at grade level beginning at the first grade, and we are restructuring our high schools to personalize instruction for students. Most important, we have developed our own online system that keeps track of individual student performance in class and on standardized tests so that the student's teachers know exactly what his or her level of progress in HISD is. With this diagnostic tool, we are able to reach more students now who otherwise might have been lost in the system.

But we know we must do more. HISD is developing a concise definition of what a dropout is and how we measure the extent of the problem. As a result, we may have a new calculation that greatly increases the number of students identified as actual dropouts. If it enables us to reach more students, so be it.

At the same time, we will work toward a reliable technology-based system that tracks where students go if they leave HISD, as well as an expanded program of dropout prevention initiatives. This must be a collaborative effort and will require guidance from the Texas Education Agency, the TEA Region IV Education Service Center, the Texas Business and Education Coalition, the Greater Houston Partnership, and other entities that truly believe we can stem the numbers of students dropping out of school. As in all HISD reforms, we cannot do this alone. Of course, major collaborators will be our students' parents, so that families become even stronger partners in students' success.

In the absence of a dropout rate and tracking system that everyone can agree on, we will also focus on increasing our graduation rate, which is the percentage of students who finish high school in four years with a diploma in hand. In HISD, our graduation rate has increased from 58.5 percent in 1998 to 68.5 percent in 2000. Our goal is to raise HISD's graduation rate to 85 percent by 2006. Clearly, we have our work cut out for us, but we believe that public school districts must be held accountable for graduating every child fully prepared to enter college or the workplace. That is our responsibility, and we accept it.

SOURCE: Reprinted with permission from Stripling, K., & Bricker, L. (2000). *HISD accepts challenge of stemming dropouts.* Retrieved July 13, 2004, from http://www.houstonisd.org

graduating, but many of them had siblings who had not completed school, and it was not uncommon for youth to leave school when they were 16 and get a job. In addition, students sensed a subtle thread of lower expectations and felt somewhat alienated from the rest of the student body—this was particularly evident at the high school level.

Committee members were pleased with the process and felt they learned valuable information that could help to inform decision making when it was time to develop or select and implement interventions or programs to increase the number of students staying in school until completion. The plan was not to pluck a program out of thin air and throw it into place. A progress report was prepared to summarize the process, document information that had been collected thus far, and propose next steps. The purpose of the committee and the reasons for addressing dropout were described, key findings were summarized, and next steps were proposed. This felt like a good time to communicate relevant information to various individuals and stakeholder groups. The community advisory group provided helpful ideas to get the message out. For example, information was communicated to the school board, through a district newsletter to parents, and in conjunction with a district-level staff workshop held in the spring. Information was well received, and input was welcomed for consideration at future committee meetings.

SUMMARY

This chapter was about making sense of the information you collected and then figuring out a way to summarize and communicate it. The importance of identifying real needs based on good information before beginning any new initiative is illustrated by a quote from a document from the Education Trust on the reporting of high school graduation rates: "It cannot be said enough that the foundation of any successful long-term improvement strategy is good information" (p. 5). If you have faithfully gathered the data and accurately interpreted your findings, you can feel confident that the foundation you have laid will be strong enough to support the work that is to come.

Now check Box 7.3 for the answers to the Myth or Truth? statements presented at the beginning of this chapter. What are your explanations for why each statement was a myth or the truth? How did your explanations match up with those provided?

REFLECTION QUESTIONS

1. The quote in the summary suggests that the foundation of any long-term improvement strategy is based on good information. What does the term *good information* mean to you?

2. How can the news media be used to effectively communicate information to the public? What strategies might work to increase the effectiveness of using the newspaper as a communication tool?

3. What are the most important contextual factors that must be in place if a new dropout prevention program is to be successful?

Box 7.3   Myth or Truth? Answers

1. **Truth.** Once you have identified your key findings, you need to analyze them to determine the root causes of the problems. *Explanation:* Sometimes the results of the information-gathering process are just symptoms of an underlying problem, not the true problem. Consequently, selecting a dropout prevention program based on findings that have not been thoroughly analyzed may result in your spending time and money trying to fix the wrong thing. (See pages 131–132.)

2. **Truth.** Prioritizing your needs based on specific criteria will help you to use your resources more effectively. *Explanation:* An information-gathering process usually produces more needs than you have the time and money to address. Prioritizing your needs will help you to decide where to start and how to spend your resources. (See page 133.)

3. **Truth.** Creating a report of your progress at this point in the process can serve many purposes. *Explanation:* Compiling all the information you have collected so far in one spot will ensure that none of the work that you have done or information you have gathered is forgotten or lost. Such a report can also serve as the basis for communicating with various audiences, justifying future decisions as well as providing a baseline of information against which progress can be measured. (See page 134.)

4. **Truth.** It is important to think carefully about the type and amount of information you should share with various stakeholder groups. *Explanation:* Too many times, information is not communicated at all or the wrong information is communicated to an audience. A communication plan will help you think through what messages you want to convey. (See page 134.)

5. **Myth.** If the information you have collected presents a less than positive picture of your school, it should not be reported to the public. *Explanation:* Although sharing what might be considered bad news is never easy, communicating the current status of your school's issues to your various audiences is a necessary step. You might soften the blow by first writing articles on the importance of using accurate data to make decisions and conveying your commitment to address whatever challenges the data might reveal. Then, after the stage is set, you can begin to candidly share the results of your information gathering process. (See page 135.)

FURTHER READING

Bernhardt, V. L. (1999). *The school portfolio: A comprehensive framework for school improvement* (2nd ed.). Larchmont, NY: Eye on Education.

Bernhardt, V. L., von Blanckensee, L. L., Lauck, M. S., Rebello, F. F., Bonilla, G. L., & Tribbey, M. M. (2000). *The example school portfolio.* Larchmont, NY: Eye on Education.

Education Trust. (2003). *Telling the whole truth (or not) about high school graduation.* Washington, DC: Author.

Preuss, P. G. (2003). *The leader's guide to root cause analysis: Using data to dissolve problems.* Larchmont, NY: Eye on Education.

Scholtes, P. R., Joiner, B. L., & Streibel, B. J. (2003). *The team handbook* (3rd ed.). Madison, WI: Oriel.

Stripling, K., & Bricker, L. (2000). *HISD accepts challenge of stemming dropouts.* Retrieved July 13, 2004, from http://www.houstonisd.org

TAKING ACTION

You have spent a lot of time collecting and analyzing information. Now you are ready to organize and use it to make good decisions about what to do about the challenges you identified.

This chapter provided information about how to manage the information you have gathered so far and make sense of it so that you can use it to make decisions. We recommended a strategy for identifying real problems, not symptoms, and stressed the importance of prioritizing your needs. We encouraged you to consider putting together a progress report that would summarize your work so far and gave you some ideas about possible messages for communicating with the school staff, parents, and the school board about what you have learned and what you might be planning.

Depending on your circumstances, there are a number of directions you can go from here. To determine what your next move should be, we recommend that you read through the statements in the left-hand column of the Guide to Action Tools on page 141, identify your most immediate needs, and then use the Action Tool listed in the right-hand column to help you meet that need. Be sure to check whether there are district or school policies or procedures that must be followed before proceeding with the activities you plan to carry out.

GUIDE TO ACTION TOOLS

What Do You Need to Know or Do?	Action Tool
Summarize the results obtained from the Action Tools and identify key findings	Action Tool 7.1: *Key Findings Summary Sheet*
Prioritize needs based on established criteria	Action Tool 7.2: *Prioritization Matrix*
Summarize the steps taken in the information-gathering process, identify the results obtained, discuss the conclusions reached, and communicate next steps	Action Tool 7.3: *Progress Report*
Communicate appropriate information to various individuals and stakeholder groups	Action Tool 7.4: *Communication Plan*

ACTION TOOL 7.1   KEY FINDINGS SUMMARY SHEET

Objective: To summarize the results obtained from the Action Tools and identify key findings

Materials: Completed Action Tools; notes

Instructions:

1. Put the name of each Action Tool you used in the first column of Action Tool 7.1: Key Findings Summary Sheet.

2. In the middle column, write a short description of the action steps you took. Include the sources of data.

3. Write the key findings from each Action Tool used.

4. Use the Five Why Method (see Chapter 4) to determine the root causes reflected in the findings.

5. Write the root causes you found in the form of statements of need for use with Action Tool 7.2.

School/District _____

ACTION TOOL 7.1   KEY FINDINGS SUMMARY SHEET

Name of Action Tool	Description of Action Taken and Sources of Data	Key Findings

ACTION TOOL 7.2   PRIORITIZATION MATRIX

Objective: To prioritize needs based on established criteria

Materials: List of identified statements of need

Instructions:

1. Generate a list of criteria to use in determining priority. Some common criteria include:
   - *Importance:* This can include how critical the need is and the potential benefit to students.
   - *Feasibility:* This can include how easily this need could be met and if meeting the need is within your control.
   - *Cost:* This can include the estimated amount of money needed as well as staff time and other resources.

2. Come to agreement on the criteria and the definitions of the criteria that you will use and put the criteria on the matrix.

3. Put all of the identified statements of need in the column titled Statements of Need.

4. Review each need and determine a point value for each criterion.

5. Total up the scores for each identified need and place the total on the matrix.

6. Rank the needs based on point totals and place the rank number on the matrix underneath the column heading Priority.

7. Discuss the prioritized list of needs and come to agreement on which needs will be addressed first. (NOTE: There could be a valid reason for selecting a priority to start with that is not your top priority according to the ranking on the Prioritization Matrix. Discuss these issues thoroughly with the action team before determining your final course of action.)

School/District _____

ACTION TOOL 7.2   PRIORITIZATION MATRIX

Statements of Need	Criteria			Total Score
	Importance 5 = High Importance	**Feasibility** 5 = High Feasibility	**Cost** 5 = Low Cost	

Priority

ACTION TOOL 7.3   PROGRESS REPORT

Objective: To summarize the steps taken in the information-gathering process, identify the results obtained, discuss the conclusions reached, and communicate next steps

Materials: Completed Action Tools from Chapters 2–6

Instructions:

1. Review the list of possible items to be included in each section of Action Tool 7.3: Progress Report, and determine which are appropriate for your report.

2. Use the results of the Action Tools to obtain the information needed for each section of the report.

3. Where appropriate, describe the process used to gather the data.

4. Attach or include documents such as news articles, staff memos, board reports, and any other supporting materials.

Follow-Up:

1. Think about various groups or individuals who should receive this report.

2. Disseminate the report to the individuals or groups identified.

School/District _____

ACTION TOOL 7.3   PROGRESS REPORT

A. Introduction

- Describe the purpose of the report and the reasons why work on dropout was initiated.
- List the names and roles of the people who have been working on the dropout issue, including how they were selected and their assigned responsibilities.
- Provide an overview of what will follow in the rest of the report.

B. Student/School/Community/Family Summary

- Describe the student population of the school by subgroup (Action Tool 3.1).
- List the number of diploma options in the school and the percentages of students by subgroup receiving each type of diploma option (Action Tool 3.2).
- List the elements of the school's definition of dropout and describe current methods for tracking students (Action Tools 3.3, 3.4, 3.5).
- Describe information gathered indicating when and why students are disengaging or dropping out (Action Tools 4.1, 4.2, 4.3, 4.4).
- Describe status and alterable risk factors at the community, school, family, and student levels (Action Tools 5.1, 5.2).
- List board policies that have implications for school completion (Action Tool 5.3).
- List content from student, parent, and teacher handbooks that has implications for school completion (Action Tool 5.4).
- Describe existing dropout prevention or early intervention programs, transition programs, and existing interventions in Grades 6–12 (Action Tools 6.1, 6.2), educational options available to students (Action Tools 6.1, 6.2), and dropout recovery programs available to students (Action Tools 6.1, 6.2).
- List the extracurricular options available to students and the percentages of students participating in those options by subgroup (Action Tool 6.3).

C. Conclusions

- Present key findings from the information collected (Action Tool 7.1).
- Describe the process used to analyze the key findings in order to determine statements of need (Action Tool 7.1).
- List the statements of need and describe the prioritization process used to determine in what order the needs will be addressed (Action Tool 7.2).

D. Next Steps

- Provide an overview of the proposed steps to be taken to select or design a dropout prevention program.

ACTION TOOL 7.4   COMMUNICATION PLAN

Objective: To communicate appropriate information to various individuals and stakeholder groups

Instructions:

1. Review the directions for designing a communication plan in Action Tool 2.5.

2. List the audiences and communication tools for this plan and enter that information in the appropriate column.

3. Generate a list of new messages such as:
   - The importance of data-based decision making
   - Key findings from the information-gathering process
   - Proposed next steps

4. For each entry on the Communication Plan, decide who should prepare the information, who should deliver the message, and when the communication task should be completed.

Follow-Up:

Once you have completed all the activities listed on your Communication Plan, consider the effectiveness of your strategies. What worked? What did not work? What will you do differently next time?

School/District _____

ACTION TOOL 7.4   COMMUNICATION PLAN

Audience	Messages	Communication Tool	Prepared by	Delivered by	Date Completed

8

Deciding
What to Do

TOPICS

- Starting From Scratch or Choosing an Existing Program
- Identifying Effective Programs
- Deciding Whether to Select or Create
- Practical Considerations for Implementation
- Ensuring Implementation Fidelity or Following the Recipe

IN THIS CHAPTER, YOU WILL . . .

- Identify pros and cons of starting from scratch or choosing an existing program
- Examine criteria for selecting an existing program
- Examine criteria for establishing a new program
- Learn about what must be considered prior to implementation
- Learn about the importance of implementing a model with fidelity

In previous chapters we have talked a great deal about why students drop out of school, what influences place students at risk of dropping out, and what kinds of programs have been used to address dropout. Now it is time to think about whether you are going to select an existing program to use or design one from scratch. It is not as easy as deciding which entrée to select from a menu—or whether you should plan and cook an entire meal. Although there are some similarities, there is much more to consider, and that is what this chapter is about. Before we get into all these decisions, read the Myth or Truth? statements in Box 8.1 and determine whether they are myths or truths. By the end of the chapter, you should know!

Box 8.1   Myth or Truth? Do You Know?

Read each statement following and decide whether it is a myth or the truth.

1. It is much easier to design your own program to address dropout than it is to choose and implement an existing one.

2. Considering the effectiveness of an existing program is critical in its selection.

3. One of the most important questions to consider when selecting an existing program is whether the program is based on a strong conceptual framework.

4. In most cases, one program will suffice to meet the needs of multiple settings regardless of match.

5. Documenting how the program was implemented will be important when it comes time to evaluate effectiveness.

STARTING FROM SCRATCH OR CHOOSING AN EXISTING PROGRAM

When charged with the responsibility of raising graduation rates and ensuring successful school completion for all students, you must decide whether to address the issue by designing a new program or choosing to implement an existing program. Designing a new program can be very time intensive—the advantage is that you can create a program that is directly aligned with your needs and available resources. Implementing an existing program may be easier because it has already been developed. The disadvantage is that it may require modifications, and there may be less personal investment in ensuring successful implementation. There are pros and cons for each choice. Some of them are listed in Table 8.1.

It is important to remember that implementing an existing program is not a simple procedure (see Box 8.2). The program may require retrofitting to ensure that

Table 8.1   Pros and Cons of Designing a New Program Versus Selecting an Existing Program

New Program	Existing Program
Pros	**Pros**
• Can be directly aligned to student, school, or district needs	• Existing materials may be available
• Those implementing the program are highly invested in its success	• May have evidence of effectiveness
	• May include advice about mistakes to avoid
	• Can consult with those who have already implemented the program
Cons	**Cons**
• Takes time, resources, and expertise to develop	• May not be successful in your setting
	• May be less personal investment in successful implementation

> **Box 8.2** Choosing an Existing Program
>
> As James McPartland, a prominent educational researcher at Johns Hopkins University notes,
>
> > It is unlikely that a program developed elsewhere can be duplicated exactly in another site, because local talents and priorities for school reform, the particular needs and interests of the students to be served, and the conditions of the school to be changed will differ. Instead of some brand-name pre-packaged, complete program to be replicated, local school reformers require a coherent set of general components to increase the holding power of schools serving students at risk, which can be adapted to fit local circumstances. (McPartland, 1995, p. 256)

it matches the needs of the students as well as the school and district where it will be implemented. If the program is to be part of a larger school reform effort, the degree to which it fits within the existing framework must also be considered.

IDENTIFYING EFFECTIVE PROGRAMS

In Chapter 6, you learned that there is no one best program for addressing school dropouts. In fact, interventions vary in approach and often use multiple strategies. Given that there are many programs to choose from, how do you know which one to select? Making the best decision is critical given the time and resources that are required for implementation. One way to determine whether to select an existing program is by reviewing information about its effectiveness. Program developers may claim program effectiveness, but it is best to use a critical eye and make an informed decision. Table 8.2 highlights key questions to ask about the effectiveness evaluation of a program.

Before selecting an intervention for implementation, you must determine whether the program was effective. This is not a simple yes or no question. The degree to which a program shows evidence of effectiveness varies along a continuum according to the rigor with which it was evaluated. You can have more confidence in

Table 8.2 Questions for Critiquing Program Effectiveness Evaluation

- Is a rigorous research or evaluation design used to determine effectiveness?
- Are statistically significant findings reported in favor of the intervention?
- Is an effect size reported, and what does it indicate?
- Are effects reported to last beyond termination of the intervention?
- Was an external evaluator used to assess program impact?
- Is information reported on the extent to which the program was implemented as intended (fidelity of implementation)?
- Has the program been effectively implemented in multiple sites?

a statement reporting that a program was effective if the evaluation incorporated key research or evaluation methodology. Critical components to consider include the research design, the significance of effects, the durability of effects, the use of an external evaluation, and whether multiple sites or studies were included.

Research Design

Programs can be evaluated in a variety of ways. The most common evaluation or research design methodologies are (1) experimental, (2) quasi-experimental, and (3) nonexperimental. *Experimental* designs randomly assign individuals to either a treatment group (the group that receives the intervention) or a control group (the group that does not receive the intervention). The use of this design provides the strongest evidence that a treatment was effective and places more confidence in attributing positive changes to the intervention. *Quasi-experimental* designs do not use random assignment, but do involve the comparison of individuals receiving the intervention with those who are not (comparison group). *Nonexperimental* designs do not use random assignment or the use of control or comparison groups. Information about the effectiveness of the intervention is gathered through the use of interviews, observations, or descriptive data. Nonexperimental studies do not provide a strong basis for making definitive statements about program effectiveness, because so many variables are not controlled.

Significance of the Effects

The magnitude of the difference between the outcomes for the individuals who received the intervention and those who did not can be measured statistically. Studies that report whether the findings were *statistically significant* provide information about whether the effects were due to chance or whether they are more likely to be attributed to the impact of the intervention. Another indicator of effectiveness is called the *effect size.* This also measures the amount of impact attributed to the program or intervention and is a measure that can give an indication of the practical significance of a difference that is found between groups after the intervention has occurred. Selection of a program that has not shown a substantial effect on individuals should be carefully considered. Box 8.3 has more information on effect size.

Durability of Effects

It is also important to know whether the effects of the intervention continued even after the intervention was discontinued. For example, suppose student attendance increased to an acceptable level during an intervention that consisted of daily feedback from an assigned adult mentor. It is important to know whether student attendance remains consistently high once the intervention ends, or if it returns to unacceptable levels. Individuals who receive the intervention should be followed over time to determine whether the effects of the intervention are long lasting. In general, the longer the effects last, the better the program impact.

Use of an External Evaluator

The use of an external evaluator is another criterion to look for when considering the quality of a research study or evaluation measuring program effectiveness.

Box 8.3 Effect Size

A statistic commonly used to measure effect size is Cohen's d, which researchers interpret as follows: $d = .2$, small effect; $d = .5$ to .8, medium effect; and $d = .8$ and higher, large effect. The statistic can be used to show the degree to which a practice, program, or policy has an effect based on research results, measured in standard deviation units.

Example: A researcher finds an effect size of $d = .5$ for an after-school tutoring program on reading achievement. This means that the average student who participates in the tutoring program will achieve one-half standard deviation above the average student who does not participate. Given a standard deviation of eight points, the effects size translates into four additional points, which might increase a students' ranking on the test.

SOURCE: Lauer, P. A. (2004). *A policymaker's primer on education research: How to understand, evaluate, and use it.* Aurora, CO: Mid-Continent Research for Education and Learning (McREL), and Denver, CO: Education Commission of the States (ECS). Retrieved March 10, 2004, from www.ecs .org/researchprimer

---

Individuals who are involved in program implementation and its evaluation are more likely to let subtle biases influence the evaluation, even if they try to guard against it. Experimental research designs that incorporate more controlled conditions are less likely to be at risk of evaluator bias.

Multiple Sites or Studies

Interventions that have been implemented in multiple sites and consistently show clear evidence of effectiveness are more likely to be considered effective than those that have only been implemented in one setting. It is important to find out whether the intervention has been replicated and determine the degree to which student outcomes improved in each application. If results vary, additional information should be gathered to understand what accounts for the differences in outcomes across settings.

DECIDING WHETHER TO SELECT OR CREATE

Now you know about some criteria to consider when examining the effectiveness of an existing program, but what if you are interested in developing your own program? Perhaps the team of people you are working with would like to establish a new program that is specifically designed to fit needs that have been identified in your setting. Table 8.3 lists questions to consider in developing a new program. These questions can also be applied when reviewing existing programs.

One of the most important questions to consider when designing or selecting an intervention to address dropout is whether the program is based on a strong conceptual framework. Is there a well-specified model underlying the program that is in existence or that is being developed? Several of the earlier chapters in this book

Table 8.3 Questions to Consider in the Selection of Existing and Design of New Programs

- Will the program be based on a conceptually sound theoretical framework?

- Will the program employ methods and strategies based on empirical research?

- Are the various components of the program aligned with the goal of the program?

- How will the program integrate successfully into the rest of the school system?

- What is the plan for ongoing, high-quality professional development for those who are implementing the program?

- Does the program include measurable goals and benchmarks for student progress towards the goal?

- Does the program provide support for teachers, administrators, and staff?

- Does the program allow for meaningful involvement by stakeholders in planning, implementing, and evaluating program activities?

- Does the program include a plan for evaluating the implementation of the program and for student results?

- Are the costs for implementing the program reasonable?

SOURCE: Adapted from *Overview of the Comprehensive School Reform Program (CSR).* (n.d.). Retrieved July 25, 2004, from http://www.ed.gov/programs/compreform/2pager.html

provided a conceptual understanding of the process of dropout. Is current research and theory being used to inform the design of the intervention? Is the theory that is being used plausible and relevant to the problem that is being addressed? Many explanations of interventions begin with a review of relevant literature and an explanation of how the intervention was developed. Interventions that do not explain their conceptual underpinnings, even if only briefly, may be suspected of being pulled out of thin air. Interventions that are based on sound theory are more apt to be successful because they are logically connected to the problem and have a rationale for how they were developed.

In addition to a strong conceptual framework, other considerations include whether various components are aligned with the goals of the program and whether the program will fit with the existing reforms that are in place. When the program is implemented, will staff development be provided? What supports will be in place to help teachers or support staff understand their role with respect to the new program? Questions about the cost of implementation and maintaining the program must also be addressed. It is important to think ahead about strategies that can be used to sustain an effective program.

If you are developing a program, think about whether you have the available expertise and capacity to undertake the project. Who will provide the leadership? Is there a strong level of commitment and support to keep things rolling? Creating a new program will require a substantial design component. How big is the project? What will it entail? How much time is available? What resources are available? Although the issues listed here are not comprehensive, suffice it to say, these kinds of questions must be carefully considered before deciding whether and how to go forward with a new initiative of your own design.

PRACTICAL CONSIDERATIONS FOR IMPLEMENTATION

So far we have been talking about the importance of examining potential interventions based on the extent to which they have a sound conceptual framework and are effective. It is also important to carefully consider key features of implementation prior to selecting a program. First and foremost, the match between the intervention and the needs of your setting must be considered. For example, suppose you are trying to address the high dropout rate for Hispanic students in an urban district. You need to ask whether the intervention you are considering was implemented with Hispanic students. Was it used in an urban setting? What modifications might need to be made to the intervention? Are cultural considerations taken into account?

In addition to assessing the match between the intervention and the needs of your setting and students, there are many other implementation features to consider. Chapter 9 addresses implementation issues in more detail. For now, attending to the implementation features listed in Table 8.4 will result in fewer headaches and unwanted surprises along the way.

ENSURING IMPLEMENTATION FIDELITY OR FOLLOWING THE RECIPE

One other important component to consider when selecting an existing intervention is the extent to which there are procedures in place to ensure that implementation will occur as intended. You must be sure you have enough information to implement it with fidelity. In some ways, this is similar to following a recipe. If you follow the recipe, it is more likely the final product will be comparable to the one that was originally created. Differences in outcomes can be accounted for by determining whether a step in the recipe was missed, or an ingredient was forgotten or replaced. Likewise, it is important to know whether an intervention has been implemented as intended in order to account for any variation in student outcomes that may occur.

Table 8.4   Implementation Considerations

- What *personnel* are required to ensure adequate implementation? Can existing personnel be used or do new employees have to be hired?
- What *training* must be provided? Who will provide the training? When will training occur, and for how long? Will ongoing training be necessary?
- What *resources* will be necessary for program implementation?
- *How long* will the intervention take to implement? Is the intervention ongoing? How will the intervention be sustained once grant monies are depleted?
- Is a *manual* available for training and implementation? Are other materials available for use (for example, curriculum, reproducible handouts)?
- What is the *cost* of the program? Is information available on costs and benefits?
- Is up-to-date *contact information* available for ongoing consultation and trouble shooting?

To begin, it is important that the intervention is clearly described and includes information about key program components. A manual that provides a thorough explanation of the program and includes examples of implementation can be especially helpful. Additionally, training sessions or ongoing staff development topics can increase the likelihood that an intervention will be implemented with fidelity.

Second, procedures or tools should be available to clearly and efficiently document who receives the intervention and how it is being delivered. For example, suppose a group of eight students are to be part of a career development class for a semester followed by a semester-long work experience. It is critical to have a way to document information about the extent to which participation occurred (how many students attended and how often), the content and delivery of the classes, and the quality of work experience. Without this information, it is difficult to determine whether lack of effectiveness is due to poor implementation of what might otherwise be an effective intervention.

An existing program should include information and a procedure specifying the data that must be collected to ensure the recipe is followed. Similarly, you will need to develop these tools if you are designing and implementing a new program or strategy to increase the numbers of students who complete school.

Implementation Scenario: Deciding What to Do (March/April/May)

Now, it was time for the nitty-gritty business of determining what strategies or programs to put into place. It was decided that this would be done on two levels. First, the district would create an overall plan to put into place in order to address some of the broader issues. Next, each of the pilot schools was asked to identify programs or interventions that could be used to reach students at the universal, indicated, and/or selected levels. All of the programs would be directly linked to the needs of the student population. If some programs were already in place and were meeting identified needs, those were included in the plan as well.

Each committee member was assigned to identify a program or strategy that could be used to address some of the needs that were relevant to the problem of dropout identified by the committee in previous meetings. Committee members were asked to examine existing programs critically using an existing worksheet with specified criteria to determine whether they were conceptually or methodologically sound. If a program was not found that was already in existence, creating a new program could be considered. The pros and cons of choosing an existing program as compared to starting a new program were discussed and reflected upon. Practical considerations were noted including cost, required support personnel, training, additional resources, and more. Finally, programs were compared with respect to the presence of a conceptual model, evidence of effectiveness, alignment with identified needs, implementation considerations, and the potential extent of program modification. To give you an example, one of the options considered by the middle school team is briefly summarized.

- *Middle School Team.* As the committee from the middle school met, they became more aware of the high frequency of fighting and student conflicts in their setting. The level of staff moral and a survey of students reflected a concern in the area of respectful student relationships. Parent input also revealed a low score on the districtwide climate survey for this particular school. Disruptive incidents interrupted student learning, and students were often suspended (as reflected in discipline records) for persistent disruptive behavior. The school identified a need to develop a safe, caring, cooperative learning environment. One of the committee members at the middle school found research showing school-based prevention programs focused on social-emotional learning resulted in improved student outcomes, including academic success and graduation. It appeared students needed to be taught skills that would help them better manage their emotions, solve problems effectively, and work cooperatively with others. Several programs that were in existence were reviewed and compared for potential selection.

SUMMARY

The decision of whether to select an existing dropout prevention program or design a new program is probably one of the more difficult and important ones you will make. We have highlighted the pros and cons of each choice. When choosing an existing program, it is important to critically evaluate its effectiveness. We have suggested questions to help guide the decision and have suggested that many of the same questions must be considered in the design of a new intervention as in the selection of an existing one.

In this chapter we also highlighted several practical considerations for implementation. Determining the extent to which the program matches the needs of your students or school and how it fits with comprehensive school reform efforts is very important. Of course, there are also questions about the cost of the program, support personnel, availability and extensiveness of training, additional required resources, and more. Finally, it is important to know what materials are available to document the extent to which the program is implemented as intended, so that evaluation information will reflect the effect of the program you intended to implement.

Now, check your answers to the Myth or Truth? statements by looking at Box 8.4. Are the explanations consistent with your understanding?

REFLECTION QUESTIONS

1. Consider the types of programs that are currently in place in your school or district to address dropout. How were these programs chosen, or how were they designed?

2. Consider the pros and cons of selecting a program versus designing your own. What would influence the choice that you make?

3. A solid conceptual foundation, evidence of effectiveness, and practical considerations for implementation must all be carefully examined when choosing a program. Which of the considerations is most important to you and why?

Box 8.4   Myth or Truth? Answers

---

1. **Myth.** It is much easier to design your own program to address dropout than it is to choose and implement an existing one. *Explanation:* There are pros and cons to both selecting an existing program and designing your own. (See page 151.)

2. **Truth.** Considering the effectiveness of an existing program is critical in its selection. *Explanation:* Given the time and resources required for implementation, selection of a program that does not have proven effectiveness could be very costly. (See page 152.)

3. **Truth.** One of the most important questions to consider when selecting an existing program is whether the program is based on a strong conceptual framework. *Explanation:* A program that is not based on a strong conceptual framework is suspect to being pulled out of thin air because someone thought it was a good idea. This is risky. (See pages 154–155.)

4. **Myth.** In most cases, one program will suffice to meet the needs of multiple settings regardless of match. *Explanation:* One program does not fit all. (See page 156.)

5. **Truth.** Documenting how the program was implemented will be important when it comes time to evaluate effectiveness. *Explanation:* Documenting the extent to which the program was implemented as intended can provide valuable information that can be related to program effectiveness and impact. (See page 157.)

FURTHER READING

Christenson, S. L., Sinclair, M. F., Lehr, C. A., & Godber, Y. (2001). Promoting successful school completion: Critical conceptual and methodological considerations. *School Psychology Quarterly, 16*(4), 468–484.

Crane, J. (Ed.). (1998). *Social programs that work.* New York: Russell Sage Foundation.

Lauer, P. A. (2004). *A policymaker's primer on education research: How to understand, evaluate, and use it.* Aurora, CO: Mid-Continent Research for Education and Learning (McREL), and Denver, CO: Education Commission of the States (ECS). Retrieved March 10, 2004, from www.ecs.org/researchprimer

McPartland, J. M. (1994). Dropout prevention in theory and practice. In R. J. Rossi (Ed.), *Schools and students at risk: Context and framework for positive change* (pp. 255–276). New York: Teachers College.

National Research Council and Institute of Medicine. (2002). *Community programs to promote youth development.* Committee on Community-Level Programs for Youth. J. Eccles & J. A. Gootman (Eds.). Board on Children, Youth and Families, Division of Behavioral and Social Sciences and Education. Washington, DC: National Academy Press.

Stringfield, S. C. (1994). Identifying and addressing organizational barriers to reform. In R. J. Rossi (Ed.), *Schools and students at risk: Context and framework for positive change* (pp. 277–295). New York: Teachers College.

TAKING ACTION

This section is for those of you who are ready to decide whether and how to select or design a program to meet your needs and increase graduation for all. First you will need to gather and analyze some information in order to make an informed decision. Action Tools to assist you are provided in this section. One of your first tasks after reading the information presented in this chapter may be to evaluate the effectiveness of an existing program that you are considering for replication. A list of criteria to assist you in your review is provided here. It will also be important to analyze programs that you are considering for implementation and compare these programs to select the one that best meets your needs. Practical issues associated with implementation must also be addressed.

Depending on your circumstances, there are a number of directions you can go from here. To determine what your next move should be, we recommend that you read through the statements in the left-hand column of the Action Tools Guide, identify your most immediate needs, and then use the Action Tool listed in the right-hand column to gather the information you need. It is important to remember that the Action Tools are sample forms that are provided to assist you in gathering and organizing data that will help you to make informed decisions about how to address dropout in your setting. The tools can be reproduced; however, they may need to be modified to meet the needs of your school or district. Be sure to check whether there are district or school policies or procedures that must be followed before proceeding with the activities you plan to carry out.

GUIDE TO ACTION TOOLS

What Do You Need to Know or Do?	Action Tool
Evaluate effectiveness of an existing program or strategy in light of key criteria	Action Tool 8.1: *Effectiveness Evaluation Form*
Consider key components for implementation	Action Tool 8.2: *Program Implementation Form*
Identify and analyze individual program strengths and weaknesses	Action Tool 8.3: *Program Analysis Form*
Determine which program to select	Action Tool 8.4: *Program Comparison Form*

ACTION TOOL 8.1 EFFECTIVENESS EVALUATION FORM

Objective: To evaluate the effectiveness of existing dropout prevention and intervention programs and strategies

Instructions:

1. Determine what program is going to be reviewed. Use a new form for each program that is reviewed.

2. Review each component listed in Action Tool 8.1. Read program descriptions, program manuals, and evaluation reports to determine the extent to which the program was effective.

3. Document findings on the form provided.

Follow-Up:

1. Review findings for each program that is evaluated and determine areas of strength and weakness. Programs with a higher number of responses indicating "yes" are viewed more favorably because they meet multiple criteria.

2. Write a statement that summarizes your findings.

School/District _____

ACTION TOOL 8.1   EFFECTIVENESS EVALUATION FORM

Summarize identified needs, overarching goals, and objectives that you are trying to address:

Title of Program to Be Reviewed

Evidence of Conceptual or Theoretical Framework	YES	NO
Describe:		
Evidence of Effectiveness		
Experimental research design	YES	NO
Quasi–experimental research design	YES	NO
Nonexperimental research design	YES	NO
Statistically significant findings in favor of intervention	YES	NO
Effect size reported in favor of intervention (Cohen's $d > .5$)	YES	NO
Effects reported to last beyond termination of intervention	YES	NO
Use of external evaluator	YES	NO
Program has been effectively implemented in multiple sites	YES	NO
Summary Statement:		

163

ACTION TOOL 8.2   PROGRAM IMPLEMENTATION FORM

Objective: To review and document critical considerations necessary for program implementation

Instructions:

1. Determine what program is going to be reviewed. Use a new form for each program that is reviewed.

2. Review each component of implementation listed in Action Tool 8.1. Read program descriptions, program manuals, and evaluation reports to determine what is required for implementation of the program.

3. Document information on Action Tool 8.2.

Follow-Up:

1. Review findings for each program that is evaluated and determine areas of strength and weakness.

2. Develop a Summary Statement after reviewing the implementation requirements for each program.

School/District _____

ACTION TOOL 8.2   PROGRAM IMPLEMENTATION FORM

Summarize identified needs, overarching goals, and objectives that you are trying to address:

Title of Program	

Support Personnel	**Comments/Notes**
Are support personnel needed to assist with program implementation?	
How many personnel will be required?	
Will personnel be hired or will existing staff be utilized?	
What are the job requirements?	

Training	**Comments/Notes**
What training is necessary?	
When will training occur and for how long?	
Will ongoing training be necessary?	
Who will provide the training?	
What resources are available for training (e.g., manual)?	
What is the cost of training?	

Additional Resources	**Comments/Notes**
Will additional resources be necessary for program start-up or continuation?	
If yes, describe.	

Duration	**Comments/Notes**
Is the duration of the program long term (more than 6 months)?	
What is the anticipated duration?	
How will the intervention be sustained over time?	

Cost	**Comments/Notes**
Does the program or strategy have associated costs?	
What is the cost of the program?	
Is cost/benefit analysis available?	

Contact Information	**Comments/Notes**
Is contact information available for consultation?	
If yes, document contact information here.	

Summary Statement:	

165

ACTION TOOL 8.3   PROGRAM ANALYSIS FORM

Objective: To summarize critical information necessary for making an informed decision about selecting a program for implementation

Instructions:

1. Determine the program that will be analyzed.

2. Gather information about the program from available manuals, evaluation reports, presentations, and so on. You may also transfer information you have already gathered using Action Tools 8.1 and 8.2.

3. Summarize and document the information that is collected.

4. Evaluate whether you believe the component is "excellent," "adequate," "low," or "does not meet." Place an X in the appropriate column. For example, a program that has been studied using an experimental design, shows significant effects, has a large effect size, has been replicated in several sites, and was evaluated using an individual external to the program would receive a rating of "excellent" in the category titled Evidence of Program Effectiveness.

Follow-Up:

Review each of the programs that have been analyzed and compare them using Action Tool 8.4.

School/District _____

ACTION TOOL 8.3 PROGRAM ANALYSIS FORM

Name of Program _____

Description _____

Component	Excellent	Adequate	Low	Does Not Meet
Conceptual Model				
Evidence of Program Effectiveness (Refer to Action Tool 8.1)				
Aligned With Identified Needs				
Implementation (Refer to Action Tool 8.2)				
Quality of Fit (Need or modification)				
Contact Information				

ACTION TOOL 8.4 PROGRAM COMPARISON FORM

Objective: To rank programs according to the degree to which they meet certain criteria for selection purposes

Instructions:

1. List the programs that have been reviewed in the left-hand column of the Action Tool.

2. For each program, rate them on a scale of 1 = low to 5 = high, indicating the extent to which the criteria are met. You may want to use information gathered from other tools in this section to help you complete these ratings.

3. Add up the total points for each program and record in the right-hand column on the Action Tool.

Follow-Up:

Review the total points listed for each program and compare results. Select a program based on the information gathered.

School/District _____

ACTION TOOL 8.4   PROGRAM COMPARISON FORM

Program Title and Description	Conceptual Model 5 = High	Evidence of Program Effectiveness 5 = High	Alignment With Identified Needs 5 = High	Implementation Considerations 5 = Reasonable	Extent of Program Modification 5 = Low	Total Points
Program A						
Program B						
Program C						
Program D						

9

Maintaining Momentum

TOPICS

- Designing an Implementation Plan
- Ensuring Fidelity of Implementation
- Providing Professional Development
- Reviewing and Revising Your Communication Plan

IN THIS CHAPTER, YOU WILL . . .

- Learn about the elements of an effective implementation plan
- Become familiar with Innovation Configuration Maps
- Consider messages that need to be conveyed to different audiences
- Find out about standards for professional development

This chapter is all about making sure that the program you selected to help raise graduation rates and ensure successful school completion for all students is going to be a success. You would think that once you had decided on what you were going to do, you could just go ahead and start working. But before you do that, there are some program implementation essentials that you should put in place before you begin. As was the case in Chapters 2 and 7, the areas we highlight here are not intended as a series of steps that you must do. And, if you do them, they do not have to be done in a certain order. Instead, we offer them as ideas to consider and recommend only that you do something if it is appropriate to your situation.

Before you begin, though, consider the Myth or Truth? statements in Box 9.1. By the time you have finished reading this chapter, you should know which are the myths and which are the truths.

> **Box 9.1** Myth or Truth? Do You Know?
>
> Read each statement following and decide whether it is a myth or the truth.
>
> 1. An implementation plan should be based on identified needs.
>
> 2. Having many people responsible for carrying out implementation activities will help ensure that the work gets done.
>
> 3. It is not necessary to consider contextual factors when designing your implementation plan.
>
> 4. An Innovation Configuration Map can help ensure that a new program is implemented with integrity.
>
> 5. Knowing the major components of the program will help guide professional development activities.

DESIGNING AN IMPLEMENTATION PLAN

Sometimes the reason that things do not go according to plan is that there never was a plan. To keep you from going off course while implementing your new program, it is a good idea to design an implementation plan. Although you may have received extensive training and have lots of manuals and other program materials, if you do not pull out the key program components and get them into an easy-to-use format that you can refer to on a regular basis, it will be difficult for you to implement and monitor the effectiveness of your new initiative.

If you decided to replicate an existing program, much of the information you need can be found in the manual or training materials provided by the developers. If you designed an intervention of your own, you will need to supply the information yourself. Either way, you need to isolate the implementation elements and get them into a plan that can be used easily by those guiding the implementation process. Essential elements of an implementation plan include:

- Need
- Activities
- Resources
- Person responsible
- Timeline
- Contextual factors

Need

The first element on your implementation plan is a clear statement of the need you are trying to address. Keeping your needs in front of you will help ensure that all the elements of your plan are aligned with your identified needs. An example of a needs alignment form from Iowa is shown in Figure 9.1.

Figure 9.1   Example Needs Alignment Form

Need #1	Over 70% of low achievers (failing one or more subjects) demonstrate poor attendance (miss school at least one day per week).
Objective	Contact students by phone and individual visits when absence is known (mornings) to encourage attendance. Establish friendship force identifying peer helpers to encourage attendance.
Staff Responsibility	Outreach Counselor
Evaluation Method	Attendance, Records Review
Expected Outcome	100% of our low achievers will improve their attendance compared to past records.
Need #2	30% of our middle school students are failing one or more subjects.
Objective	Provide individual tutoring assistance for all students using four strategies: (1) before and after school tutoring; (2) Saturday tutoring; (3) study hall instructor assistance; and (4) peer helper program
Staff Responsibility	Extended Staff Contract, All, Staff Counselor
Evaluation Method	Grades, Records, Standardized Testing (ITBS) (ITED)
Expected Outcome	100% of the students failing one or more subjects will improve their grades to passing.
Need #3	100% of our graduates not going on to post-secondary training and who needed support assistance to graduate did so in the past without developing a career plan.
Objective	Conduct a career planning course, including individual counseling, employment service assistance, and work experience.
Staff Responsibility	Work experience coordinator
Evaluation Method	Portfolios including Individual Career Plans
Expected Outcome	100% of our graduates needing support assistance to graduate will have completed a career portfolio that can be used to seek employment. The portfolio will include a personal career plan using the Individual Career Initiatives format.
Need #4	70% of our high school teaching staff indicate that they do not feel adequately trained to handle difficult children.
Objective	All staff at the high school level will complete 18 hours of training during the next year, utilizing video tapes and individual printed materials on how to handle difficult students. The training will be coordinated through the local university.
Staff Responsibility	Curriculum Coordinator
Evaluation Method	Records of Completion, Informal Survey of Staff
Expected Outcome	100% of the teachers will express increased confidence in handling difficult students. Additional needs for training will be identified.

SOURCE: *Example format for aligning needs, objectives, staff responsibilities, evaluation, and expected outcomes.* (n.d.) Retrieved July 1, 2004, from http://www.state.ia.us/educate/. Reprinted with permission from Iowa Department of Education, Bureau of Instructional Services, Grimes State Office Building, Des Moines, IA 50319–0146.

Activities

The next step is to describe the activities you plan to carry out to address the identified need. This is where you list every step you plan to take to achieve the results you desire. The activities you identify will be specific to your needs, but here are some examples of how those activities could be stated on your implementation plan:

- Hire a coordinator
- Provide professional development for teachers and administrators
- Gather baseline information on the target audience
- Conduct a survey of parents

Although you can word your activity statements any way you choose, note that the examples all start with verbs. Putting action words at the beginning of each statement helps you to be clear about exactly what you are supposed to do to carry out that activity.

Resources

Once you are clear about the activities that you are going to carry out, it is important to supply information about the resources you plan to use to support those activities. In addition to money—both new funds and reallocation of existing dollars—the resources you list here should also include equipment, staff time, space, and other supports necessary to ensure the program's success.

Person Responsible

The next step is to assign responsibility for carrying out each task to someone. If an activity requires more than one person to carry it out, list the names of all the people who will work on that task. Still, designate someone as the lead. Making sure that you have one "go to" person makes it easier to monitor progress and ensure that the work does not fall through the cracks because people on the team think that someone else is doing it.

Timeline

Another implementation essential is assigning a timeline to each activity. Include both start dates and end dates. Doing so not only guides your work, it also allows you to look at the timeline for all the activities as a whole, to determine whether what you are proposing is manageable.

Contextual Factors

If you used the readiness questionnaire in Chapter 2, you identified some of the factors that might inhibit the success of a new initiative. Now is the time to revisit that list and determine whether there are any factors that might get in the way of implementing the program you selected. Two factors that may limit the success of a new program are the strength of the system in which the new program will be embedded and the quality of the social relationships among the individuals in the system. Putting a new program into a dysfunctional school system is a little bit like putting a new fish in a faulty fish tank with problematic tank mates. In this situation, if the new arrival struggles and dies, we assume that there was something wrong with the fish, when in reality the problems rested with the quality of the water and the other occupants of the fish tank.

If you think there are problems in the system or difficulties among people that will negatively impact your new program, you might consider forming collegial study groups around topics that address improving the quality of your school system or social relationships, or conducting a comprehensive school improvement process. Ideas for books that you can use as the centerpiece of collegial study groups on these topics, along with information about school improvement processes, are in the Further Reading section at the end of this chapter.

There are other elements that you can include in an implementation plan. There are also many ways to format a plan. An example of an action plan from a district in Ohio that includes some different elements is shown in Figure 9.2.

ENSURING FIDELITY OF IMPLEMENTATION

We discussed fidelity of implementation in Chapter 8. Because it is so important, and can mean the difference between success and failure, it is important to mention again. One of the reasons for less than ideal results or outright failure of an initiative is that the implementers are not clear about what the critical elements of the proposed change look like in practice.

To reduce variability in implementation, consider using a tool called an Innovation Configuration (IC) Map. An Innovation Configuration Map is a written description of the important components of a program displayed on a continuum, with the ideal practice at one end of the continuum and the unacceptable or least effective practice at the other. Intermediate steps describing the practices necessary to move from least effective to ideal are located in between the two ends.

The concept of an IC grew out of studies conducted by Shirley Hord and others on the implementation of new programs or innovations. They discovered that individuals varied widely in the way they implemented what was supposed to be the same program. To counter that, Hord and her colleagues invented Innovation Configuration Maps to help users implement innovations consistently and effectively. Although developing an IC of the components of your new dropout prevention program will not ensure success, having one can help prevent some implementation problems.

If you decide to design an IC, here are some suggestions to get you started. First make a list of the major components of the program you are going to implement. If you are adopting a program, then you can use the training materials or the program manual to identify the important components. If you are implementing an intervention that you designed, then you will need to generate the list of major components of the innovation yourself. For example, you may have decided to implement a dropout prevention program in which the role of the student coordinator is a major component and there are specific responsibilities for working with families, school staff, and students. In this scenario, the role of the student coordinator would be the component, and the three subcomponents would be working with the family, working with school staff, and working with students.

Figure 9.2 Sample Action Plan

Goal: To improve our graduation rate and prepare our graduates for successful entry into higher education and/or the workforce

Performance Indicator: We will increase our graduation rate by 6% in each of the next three years and meet the graduation standard by the 2005–2006 school year.

Improvement Strategy: We will reduce the dropout rate in the district, thereby increasing our graduation rate.

ACTION PLAN				
Tasks	Responsibilities	Resources	Timeline	Process Indicators
Review our new attendance policy to determine its impact on our dropout rate	Policy committee; principals; personnel supervisor	General Fund	Ongoing	Compare number of expulsions due to attendance. Report Card Data dropout rate and attendance (building specific)
Evaluate the effectiveness of our current programs designed to serve at-risk students	Career-technical coordinators; directors; principals; classroom teachers; coordinator of alternative programming	Alternative Programming Grant; Title I; Title VI; General Fund; Safe Schools Grant; Perkins Grant	Ongoing	Programs for at-risk students are targeted for periodic review; criteria for program review are identified and standardized; effects of each program on student achievement, graduation, and attendance are monitored and measured
Determine the advisability of expanding services for students not successful in our traditional program	Board of education; cabinet; administrators; classroom teachers	General Fund; Alternative Programming Grant	Ongoing	Potential sites identified; key program components identified
Analyze current data to determine what factors are most highly associated with school dropout in our district	Career-technical coordinator; guidance counselors; principals; classroom teachers; ESP personnel; coordinator of alternative programming	General Fund	Ongoing	A process for early identification of at-risk students is developed

Improvement Strategy Evaluation: State Report Card data and EMIS data will be reviewed annually to determine our graduation and dropout rate and compare the improvement with the standard unit of measure indicated by the state

SOURCE: South-Western City Schools. *SWCS continuous improvement plan 2002–2003.* (n.d.). Retrieved July 1, 2004, from http://www.swcs.k12.oh.us/. Adapted with permission from South-Western City School, Grove City, OH 43123.

The next step is to take each subcomponent, visualize what the people would be doing who are carrying out that component, and then write a word picture of what their actions would look like if implemented in an ideal way. That description would be placed at the left end of a continuum. Next, write a description of the least desirable or unacceptable version of that subcomponent and place that information at the right end of the continuum. The last step is to write down less than ideal but acceptable variations of that subcomponent and put them in the middle of the continuum. An example of a completed Innovation Configuration Map is shown in Figure 9.3.

Once ICs are developed for each component of your program, they can be used to help individuals implementing the program to see what they are supposed to do. They also can be used to target needed staff development. If the model is being

Figure 9.3   Sample Innovation Configuration Map

Component: Role of Student Coordinator			
Subcomponent: Working With the Family			
Ideal (Level 1) Coordinator makes regular contact with the family by phone and conducts regular home visits to share information about student's behavior, provides strategies for reducing the student's risks of dropping out, and assists the family to develop problem-solving skills	**(Level 2)** Coordinator makes frequent contact with the family either by phone or through home visits to share information on student's behavior and provides strategies for reducing the student's risk of dropping out	**(Level 3)** Coordinator makes occasional contact with the family by phone to share information about student's behavior	**Unacceptable (Level 4)** Coordinator does not contact the family
Subcomponent: Working With School Staff			
Ideal (Level 1) Coordinator meets regularly with all of the student's teachers to gather and share information about student progress and collaborates on a routine basis with other adults in the school on providing strategies for increasing student's engagement with school	**(Level 2)** Coordinator meets frequently with some of the student's teachers to gather and share information about student progress and collaborates frequently with some of the other adults in the school on providing strategies for increasing student's engagement with school	**(Level 3)** Coordinator meets occasionally with a few of the student's teachers and other adults in the school to gather and share information about student progress	**Unacceptable (Level 4)** Coordinator does not meet with the student's teachers or other adults in the school
Subcomponent: Working With Students			
Ideal (Level 1) Coordinator meets regularly with the student to provide feedback about overall progress in school and specific risk factors, to discuss strategies for making progress and reducing risk factors, and to assist the student to develop plans for improvement	**(Level 2)** Coordinator meets frequently with the student to provide feedback about overall progress in school and specific risk factors and to discuss strategies for making progress and reducing risk factors	**(Level 3)** Coordinator meets occasionally with the student to provide feedback about overall progress in school	**Unacceptable (Level 4)** Coordinator does not meet with the student

implemented across several buildings or classrooms, ICs can help to ensure that the components are being consistently interpreted by everyone involved.

PROVIDING PROFESSIONAL DEVELOPMENT

In Chapter 2, we suggested that you consider providing preliminary professional development activities for staff in anticipation of the work that was to come. Because you did not know how you would be solving the dropout problem at that time, the professional development activities were limited to general topics such as understanding adolescent mental health needs and differentiating instruction to increase student learning.

Now that you have decided on a program, providing professional development for staff needs to be specific to the demands of your program. If you are adopting a program that has been used in other places, there most likely is a training component that accompanies the program. If not, or if you have designed a dropout prevention program of your own, then you should think more carefully about how to spend your professional development time and money. One way to do that is to analyze the components of the program to determine what skills and abilities staff need to implement or support the program.

Once you know what your staff development needs are, you can frame them as goals and design a professional development plan to achieve those goals. Common elements in a professional development plan are very much like the elements of the implementation plan: goal statement, description of the activities you plan to carry out to reach that goal, timeline, resources required, and person responsible for managing that activity.

For additional ideas about the design and implementation of professional development activities, review the professional development standards from the National Staff Development Council. These standards take into account the organizational *context* in which professional development opportunities are to be provided, the *process* of delivering those opportunities, and the *content* that must be embedded in professional development activities (see Figure 9.4).

REVIEWING AND REVISING YOUR COMMUNICATION PLAN

You are at the point of another opportunity to review your communication plan and revise it. If you have been using your communication planning tool all along, then you know what you need to do. Just think about the messages that should be communicated, the audiences and the messages they need to hear, and the best methods for disseminating the information to those audiences.

Note that in previous communication plans, you were conveying messages that were more general in nature. For example, you were telling people that your school had a dropout problem that you wanted to solve, and you were giving the results of your information gathering efforts. Now you know what you are going to do about solving the problem, so the messages you convey will probably be much more specific. An example of a California superintendent's message to the community about his district's plans to solve its dropout problem is contained in Box 9.2.

Figure 9.4   National Staff Development Council's Professional Development Standards

CONTEXT STANDARDS	PROCESS STANDARDS	CONTENT STANDARDS
Learning Communities: Staff development that improves the learning of all students organizes adults into learning communities whose goals are aligned with those of the school and district. **Leadership:** Staff development that improves the learning of all students requires skillful school and district leaders who guide continuous instructional improvement. **Resources:** Staff development that improves the learning of all students requires resources to support adult learning and collaboration.	**Data-Driven:** Staff development that improves the learning of all students uses disaggregated student data to determine adult learning priorities, monitor progress, and help sustain continuous improvement. **Evaluation:** Staff development that improves the learning of all students uses multiple sources of information to guide improvement and demonstrate its impact. **Research-Based:** Staff development that improves the learning of all students prepares educators to apply research to decision making. **Design:** Staff development that improves the learning of all students uses learning strategies appropriate to the intended goal. **Learning:** Staff development that improves the learning of all students applies knowledge about human learning and change. **Collaboration:** Staff development that improves the learning of all students provides educators with the knowledge and skills to collaborate.	**Equity:** Staff development that improves the learning of all students prepares educators to understand and appreciate all students, create safe, orderly and supportive learning environments, and hold high expectations for their academic achievement. **Quality Teaching:** Staff development that improves the learning of all students deepens educators' content knowledge, provides them with research-based instructional strategies to assist students in meeting rigorous academic standards, and prepares them to use various types of classroom assessments appropriately. **Family Involvement:** Staff development that improves the learning of all students provides educators with knowledge and skills to involve families and other stakeholders

SOURCE: *Standards for staff development* (Rev. ed.). (2001). Oxford, OH: National Staff Development Council. Reprinted with permission of the National Staff Development Council, www.nsdc.org, 2004. All rights reserved.

Now is also a good time to revisit the list of other groups working in areas related to dropout prevention that you generated in Chapter 2 and determine how you might share information with them about what you are planning. Connecting new initiatives with existing efforts will help your project become and be seen as an integrated part of the whole system, rather than as an unrelated "add-on" relegated to the margins of your school.

Implementation Scenario: Maintaining Momentum (May)

Committee members (at district and school levels) were excited to have specific ideas about what they wanted to put in place. However, before moving to implementation, the committee chair suggested they step back for a moment and take the time to gather their thoughts and get organized. After discussion, the committee members agreed that this would be critical in order to get started on the right foot— and would increase chances for success. Members of the committee were assigned

Box 9.2   Superintendent's Message: A Multiprong Approach to Decreasing
               Dropouts

Like school systems throughout the nation, the Sweetwater Union High School District
strives to keep students from calling it quits and leaving high school before graduation.
That's why we are becoming more aggressive than ever in supporting students who are
potential dropouts and why we are launching what is possibly the most integrated, most
strategic approach to student retention in San Diego county.

Our approach is three-pronged. The first element—which comes only after a thorough
assessment of students' needs—involves teaching students new skills that help them
become more effective in both the academic and social arenas. For example, students
who are identified as potential dropouts might receive training in coping techniques, time
management, study tactics, making and keeping commitments, or conflict resolution.

Integrated support is the second component. The at-risk youth is paired with an adult
mentor, receives peer resources (such as mentor or tutor), and participates in a student
support group led by a staff member. This triple-layer of support provides effective guidance, encouragement, and positive reinforcement. These partners and support systems
help struggling students more successfully address challenges, cope with disappoint-
ments, and make wise decisions in academic and social issues.

Also in the equation is bonding—engaging the students in school activities that create
a relationship between them and their campus community. School staff members help
students select activities and programs that interest them. Whether they join athletics, a
student club, or an after-school program, their involvement makes school more appeal-
ing and helps cultivate a desire to be on campus with their peers.

This kind of multifaceted intervention offers a powerful dose of reinforcement for
students who are headed toward a premature exit from school. Coupled with an extensive alternative education program and the variety of educational options that are available throughout the district, Sweetwater's dropout prevention program should increase
graduation rates and help higher percentages of students earn high school diplomas.

SOURCE: *A multiprong approach to decreasing dropouts.* (1998). Retrieved July 15, 2004, from
http://www.suhsd.k12.ca.us. Reprinted with permission from Edward M. Brand, EdD, Superintendent, Sweetwater Union High School District, Chula Vista, CA.

the task of designing an implementation plan. Each of the representatives from the
elementary, middle, and high schools went back to their respective school-level committees and went through the process of completing an implementation plan. These
plans served as blueprints to help identify the activities that would be required to
meet the identified needs, determine the necessary resources, identify who would be
responsible for overseeing the implementation of the activity, and establish timelines
with a designated start and end date. In addition, each of the committees scheduled
additional meeting times throughout the following year to revisit the implementation plans to ensure they were being followed, reflect on progress, and make any
necessary adjustments.

The middle school committee decided to utilize a strategy that would help to
ensure the intervention they had chosen would be implemented as intended and
with fidelity. They identified factors associated with successful implementation of
the evidence-based social-emotional learning program they identified for use. For
example, the presence of a coordinator to oversee implementation, ongoing training,
consistent support from those in leadership positions, and varied and engaging

instructional approaches were all discussed. The committee decided to create an Innovation Configuration Map, and specified descriptions or scenarios reflecting implementation along a continuum ranging from unacceptable to acceptable. This was a very concrete way to communicate an understanding of what the desired implementation would look like.

SUMMARY

So far you have been gaining an understanding of the issues related to preventing dropout and how your school is doing on those issues. You have asked questions, found answers, and made decisions. Now you need to make sure that all your hard work is not wasted. In this chapter we talked about taking steps to ensure that this does not happen. We outlined strategies for designing an implementation plan and ensuring fidelity of implementation. We offered suggestions for providing professional development and revising your communication plan. These ideas and suggestions should help you to maintain momentum as you prepare to implement your program.

Now check the answers to the Myth or Truth? statements presented at the beginning of this chapter. What are your explanations for why each statement was a myth or the truth? How did your explanations match up with those provided?

Box 9.3   Myth or Truth? Answers

1. **Truth.** An implementation plan should be based on identified needs. *Explanation:* The needs you identified form the basis of your implementation plan. Every element of the plan, such as activities, resources, and evaluation methods, should be aligned with the needs. (See page 171.)

2. **Myth.** Having many people responsible for carrying out implementation activities will help ensure that the work gets done. *Explanation:* Although it is helpful to have many people working together to implement the activities, assigning one person the lead responsibility for ensuring that the work is done will ensure that tasks do not fall through the cracks because people think that someone else is doing them. (See page 173.)

3. **Myth.** It is not necessary to consider contextual factors when designing your implementation plan. *Explanation:* Some contextual factors can inhibit the success of your program while other factors can enhance your work. Identifying both barriers and assets when writing your implementation plan will help you to capitalize on your strengths and minimize or eliminate your challenges. (See pages 173–174.)

4. **Truth.** An Innovation Configuration Map can help ensure that a new program is implemented with integrity. *Explanation:* Innovation Configuration Maps clearly specify what the proposed change will look like in practice. Knowing what is ideal, as well as what is unacceptable, will help to ensure fidelity of implementation. (See pages 174–176.)

5. **Truth.** Knowing the major components of the program will help guide professional development activities. *Explanation:* Most new educational initiatives require that those implementing the initiative acquire new skills. Analyzing the components of the program to determine what skills and abilities staff will need can help you make good decisions about what professional development opportunities to provide. (See page 177.)

REFLECTION QUESTIONS

1. Describe organizational barriers that can prevent new initiatives from succeeding. What ideas do you have about how those barriers can be removed?

2. What are the advantages and disadvantages of using an Innovation Configuration Map to monitor the implementation of a new program? Are there other situations in which Innovation Configuration Maps can be used?

3. Why might the professional development standards of the National Staff Development Council be relevant to your dropout prevention efforts?

FURTHER READING

American Institutes for Research. (1999). *An educators' guide to schoolwide reform.* Arlington, VA: Educational Research Service.

Atkinson, A. J. (2003). *Planning for results: The complete guide for planning and evaluating safe and drug-free schools and communities act programs.* Richmond, VA: Greystone Publishers.

Barth, R. S. (1990). *Improving schools from within: Teachers, parents, and principals can make the difference.* San Francisco, CA: Jossey-Bass.

Brand, E. M. (1998). *A multiprong approach to decreasing dropouts.* Retrieved July 15, 2004, from http://www.suhsd.k12.ca.us

Bryk, A. S., & Schneider, B. L. (2002). *Trust in schools: A core resource for improvement.* New York: Russell Sage Foundation.

Dufour, R., & Eaker, R. E. (1998). *Professional learning communities at work: Best practices for enhancing student achievement.* Bloomington, IN: National Educational Service.

Hall, G. E., & Hord, S. M. (2001). *Implementing change: Patterns, principles, and potholes.* Needham, MA: Allyn & Bacon.

Hord, S. M., Rutherford, W. L., Huling-Austin, L. L., & Hall, G. E. (1987). *Taking charge of change.* Alexandria, VA: Association for Supervision and Curriculum Development.

Iowa State Department of Education. (n.d.). *Example format for aligning needs, objectives, staff responsibilities, evaluation, and expected outcomes.* Retrieved July 1, 2004, from http://www.state.ia.us/educate/

National Staff Development Council (NSDC). (2001). *Standards for staff development* (rev. ed.). Oxford, OH: Author.

National Staff Development Council (NSDC). (2003). *Moving NSDC's staff development standards into practice: Innovation configurations.* Oxford, OH: Author.

South-Western City Schools. *SWCS continuous improvement plan 2002–2003.* (n.d.). Retrieved July 1, 2004, from http://www.swcs.k12.oh.us/

TAKING ACTION

You are almost ready to actually start doing something to stem the tide of dropouts in your school. But before you take action, there are some things you can do to put any course of action you select on solid ground and maintain momentum once you start.

This chapter provided an opportunity for you to collect your thoughts and get organized before starting the implementation phase. We outlined elements essential to ensuring that your new initiative will be a success, including tips on developing an implementation plan and how to design Innovation Configuration Maps that will help you implement your new program or model with integrity. We suggested that you revisit your communication plan in order to bring your various stakeholder groups up to date and encouraged you to pay special attention to the importance of providing sufficient professional development opportunities for staff.

Depending on your circumstances, there are a number of directions you can go from here. To determine what your next move should be, we recommend that you read through the statements in the left-hand column of the Guide to Action Tools, identify your most immediate needs, and then use the Action Tool listed in the right-hand column to help you meet that need. Be sure to check whether there are district or school policies or procedures that must be followed before proceeding with the activities you plan to carry out.

GUIDE TO ACTION TOOLS

What Do You Need to Know or Do?	Action Tool
Design a plan to guide the implementation process	Action Tool 9.1: *Implementation Plan*
Create a written description of the program to ensure that the intervention is implemented consistently and according to the developer's specifications	Action Tool 9.2: *Innovation Configuration Map*
Design a plan for implementing professional development activities	Action Tool 9.3: *Professional Development Plan*
Communicate appropriate information to various individuals and stakeholder groups	Action Tool 9.4: *Communication Plan*

ACTION TOOL 9.1   IMPLEMENTATION PLAN

Objective: To design a plan to guide the implementation process

Instructions:

1. Enter the identified need on the Action Tool.

2. List the activities necessary to address that need. (NOTE: Starting each activity with a verb will help specify exactly what you are supposed to do.)

3. List the resources needed to support the activities. (NOTE: Besides entering the amount of money required, you may also wish to indicate if these are new funds or a reallocation of existing funds. In either case, it may be a good idea to list the source of the funding as well as the amount. In addition to monetary resources, list staff, equipment, and space resources.)

4. Assign an individual the responsibility of overseeing the implementation of each activity. (NOTE: If a team is assigned the responsibility of working on an activity, list all names but assign one person the lead role and put an asterisk by that person's name.)

5. Determine the start date and end date for each activity.

6. List contextual factors that may inhibit or enhance the implementation process.

Follow-Up:

1. Although you have assigned the responsibility for carrying out tasks to various people, who is responsible for managing the entire implementation plan?

2. How often do you plan to revisit the implementation plan in order to make necessary adjustments?

3. How will you address the contextual factors that are barriers? How will you build on the assets?

School/District _____

ACTION TOOL 9.1   IMPLEMENTATION PLAN

Need	Activities	Resources	Person Responsible	Timeline

Contextual Factors:

ACTION TOOL 9.2   INNOVATION CONFIGURATION MAP

Objective: To create a written description of the program to ensure that the intervention is implemented consistently and according to the developer's specifications

Instructions:

1. Take one major component of the program.

2. Identify subcomponents under that component and visualize what those implementing the program or model would be doing if their actions were implemented in an ideal way.

3. Place that word description on the Innovation Configuration (IC) Map in the column marked Ideal.

4. Think about what those implementing that subcomponent would be doing (or not doing) if their actions were unacceptable. Place that word description on the Innovation Configuration Map in the column marked Unacceptable.

5. Write variations of the subcomponent that are less than ideal yet acceptable, and place those variations in the Innovation Configuration Map in the columns marked Level 2 and Level 3.

6. Share the Innovation Configuration Map with those who are implementing the program, get their feedback, and revise the IC accordingly.

School/District _____

ACTION TOOL 9.2   INNOVATION CONFIGURATION MAP

Component:

Subcomponent: _____			
Ideal (Level 1)	(Level 2)	(Level 3)	Unacceptable (Level 4)
Subcomponent: _____			
Ideal (Level 1)	(Level 2)	(Level 3)	Unacceptable (Level 4)
Subcomponent: _____			
Ideal (Level 1)	(Level 2)	(Level 3)	Unacceptable (Level 4)
Subcomponent: _____			
Ideal (Level 1)	(Level 2)	(Level 3)	Unacceptable (Level 4)

ACTION TOOL 9.3   PROFESSIONAL DEVELOPMENT PLAN

Objective: To design a plan for implementing professional development activities

Materials: Program training guide

Instructions:

1. If you are adopting an existing dropout prevention program, use the materials provided by the developer to identify the goals for your professional development plan. If you do not have access to already prepared training materials, identify the skills and abilities needed by staff, and then write those needs as goals.

2. Enter your goals on the Action Tool and then identify the specific content of what people will learn as well as how they will learn it and put that information in the column marked Activities.

3. Enter the start and end dates of the activity in the column marked Timeline. Include the total number of hours or days of training.

4. Determine the resources required (money as well as time, equipment, and facilities), and enter that information in the column marked Resources Required.

5. Identify the name of the individual responsible for ensuring that the professional development activity takes place, and enter that information in the column marked Person Responsible.

Follow-Up:

1. What indicators will you accept that the professional development activity was a success?

2. How do you plan to gather information on these indicators?

3. How do you plan to convey the results of your professional development efforts to others?

School/District _____

ACTION TOOL 9.3 PROFESSIONAL DEVELOPMENT PLAN

Goal	Activities	Timeline	Resource Required	Person Responsible

ACTION TOOL 9.4   COMMUNICATION PLAN

Objective: To communicate appropriate information to various individuals and stakeholder groups

Instructions:

1. Review the directions for designing a communication plan in Action Tool 2.5.

2. List the audiences and communication tools for this plan and enter that information in the appropriate column on Action Tool 9.4.

3. Generate a list of new messages such as:
   - Intended plans for solving the dropout problem
   - Hiring or reassigning staff
   - Professional development activities planned for staff
   - Role of parents and the community in carrying out the new initiative

4. For each entry on the Communication Plan, decide who should prepare the information, who should deliver the message, and when the communication task should be completed.

Follow-Up:

Once you have completed all the activities listed on your Communication Plan, consider the effectiveness of your strategies. What worked? What did not work? What will you do differently next time?

School/District _____

ACTION TOOL 9.4   COMMUNICATION PLAN

Audience	Messages	Communication Tool	Prepared by	Delivered by	Date Completed

10

Evaluating Effectiveness

TOPICS

- The Importance of Evaluation
- What to Measure
- When to Measure
- How to Measure
- Critical Considerations in Definitions and Calculations

IN THIS CHAPTER, YOU WILL . . .

- Learn about the importance of evaluating your efforts
- Consider what to measure for the evaluation
- Learn about formative and summative evaluation
- Examine how to measure results for evaluation purposes
- Identify critical considerations in measuring improvement

Evaluating our intervention efforts is just as important as doing the interventions! So, in this chapter we give you information on what, when, and how to measure results. Evaluating the program that you have designed or selected is an important step, because you must have an objective measure of its impact. You must be able to answer whether more students were engaged in school and graduated as a result of your program.

Read the Myth or Truth? statements for this chapter in Box 10.1 and determine whether each is a myth or truth. The answers are provided at the end of the chapter.

> **Box 10.1   Myth or Truth? Do You Know?**
>
> Read each statement following and decide whether it is a myth or the truth.
>
> 1. Evaluating the effectiveness of your program is the least important part of your implementation plan.
>
> 2. Evaluation can be conducted during implementation and used to help modify things along the way.
>
> 3. Unintended consequences that occur during the implementation process should be ignored because they are not part of your objective.
>
> 4. Summative evaluation typically occurs at the end of a program and focuses on measuring impact.
>
> 5. Checklists, surveys, tests, interviews, and observations can all be used as evaluation tools.

THE IMPORTANCE OF EVALUATION

Evaluating the impact of programs to decrease the number of students dropping out of school is critical. Often, this component is given the least time and attention, and sometimes it is forgotten altogether. After spending the time and energy on getting your program going, there may be few resources left to evaluate results, whether the resources are energy, time, staff, or money. One way to guard against the lack of resources at the end is to build the evaluation into the implementation plan from the beginning. To do so, you need to argue for the evaluation from the beginning. Some of the most important reasons to conduct an evaluation include:

- *To determine effectiveness of the intervention.* Although this is an obvious reason, it is often overlooked! A statement about the effectiveness of a program cannot be made if an evaluation does not occur. The more rigorous and methodologically sound the evaluation, the more confident you can be in attributing results to the intervention.
- *To help make data-based decisions and modifications to improve effectiveness during implementation.* Suppose a program is funded for three years. If program outcomes are measured during Year 3 only, opportunities for improvement along the way will be lost. In contrast, ongoing evaluation can provide important information about changes that may need to be made along the way. Continued monitoring can measure the effectiveness of modifications that are incorporated.
- *To provide a rationale for continued funding.* Clear evidence of effectiveness gathered through an evaluation can be a powerful strategy to receive continued funding for a new program.
- *To help other educators and policymakers learn about effective practices.* Evaluation results can be used to document effective practices for others and help them make informed decisions about strategies and programs that can decrease dropout.

WHAT TO MEASURE

Identifying what to measure is a critical first step in an evaluation. Impact on outcomes associated with graduation and dropout are a likely focus here. Depending on the specific program goals, objectives, and needs, it will be important to measure indicators associated with dropout as well as enrollment status itself, such as graduation rate. These data are more powerful in attributing positive change to the intervention when they are collected for students who are receiving the intervention, as well as for a similar population of students who have not received the intervention (a control or comparison group). In addition, when possible, it is important to collect and review data from several years prior to the intervention to determine any pre-existing trends. Box 10.2 lists indicators linked to dropout that could be measured to determine program impact.

Many studies of program effectiveness measure factors associated with dropout and school completion. For example, a program designed to decrease dropout rates implements a tutoring program for eighth grade students who have low reading test scores. If the evaluation only measured change in reading test scores, but did not follow the students to determine whether they actually graduated, it would not have done enough. Measurement of enrollment status—usually dropout or graduation rates—is critical if the overarching goal of the program is to affect school completion. Measurement of this variable would require persistent efforts to follow cohorts of students or individual students over time, but would be essential.

Evaluators must also consider whether the outcomes to be measured are qualitative or quantitative. *Qualitative data* generally consist of narrative description or observation, while *quantitative outcomes* generally take the form of numerical data. It is often useful to measure in both qualitative and quantitative ways. The decision you make will have implications for the tools you use, how information is analyzed, and how it is reported. For example, to determine the impact of a program on

---

Box 10.2   What to Measure: Indicators Associated With Dropout or School Completion

The number and types of indicators that are measured to determine progress toward increasing school completion will vary for each setting due to unique circumstances. It is best to track those indicators that have been strongly associated with dropout in your school or district. The following is a list of potential indicators associated with dropout or school completion to give you an idea of what might be measured:

- Percentage of students involved in extracurricular activities
- Average percentage daily attendance
- Percentage of students receiving out-of-school suspension
- Percentage of students receiving passing grades
- Percentage of students completing homework assignments on time
- Average score on a scale assessing school bonding
- Ratings of school climate
- Percentile scores on reading tests
- Attitude toward school and learning
- Credits earned on average

student attendance, it may be useful to gather data on percentage of daily attendance over time, and it may also be useful to interview students to capture more detailed information about their perceptions of how the program helped or did not help them improve their attendance.

Another aspect of deciding what to measure includes purposeful attention to measuring unintended consequences or results of program implementation. Measurement of these kinds of outcomes may emerge as program implementation occurs. These unintended outcomes may prove valuable in assessing program impact or help to provide information about how to modify a program to avoid undesirable unintended consequences, or they may help a program determine how to increase desirable unintended outcomes. For example, suppose a tutoring program is implemented using individuals from a local company as tutors to assist middle school students who require additional reading assistance. One unintended consequence of this strategy might be increased knowledge and student exposure to outside career possibilities and recognition of the importance of obtaining a high school diploma. This unintended consequence might best be measured and reported in a qualitative manner. Regardless of how captured, it is important to capture the unexpected impact.

Last, when considering what to measure, it is important to measure the extent to which the program was implemented as intended. This concept of following the recipe was discussed in Chapter 8. Although it is difficult to implement interventions in applied situations as exact replications with attention to every detail, systematic attempts increase the chances that the intervention will be implemented as intended. Systematic documentation of how implementation occurs will be unique to each type of program. However, it can and should be measured for each strategy or program that is implemented.

WHEN TO MEASURE

Evaluations measure program implementation and impact in two ways: (1) throughout implementation, usually at predetermined intervals, and (2) at the end of the program. Both types of evaluation are important for dropout intervention programs.

The first type of evaluation is usually referred to as "formative evaluation." For example, in this type of evaluation the implementation and impact of a three-year program may be documented and measured twice each year, perhaps in the fall and in the spring of each academic year. This type of evaluation is used to determine what is going well and what might need improvement or added attention as implementation occurs. During a formative evaluation, what is actually occurring may be compared with the program's objectives and timeline. In addition, the manner in which the program is delivered could be measured over time (one way of documenting fidelity of implementation). As the information is being gathered, it can be used to inform individuals of the need for modification if necessary. For example, a homework help group may be offered as a strategy to keep students on track to graduate. However, as evaluation data are gathered, it is noted that few students are showing up for the additional assistance. After talking with students, it is determined that the help is offered at the same time as after-school sports, and many students are not aware of the new program that is being offered. This information may then be used to strengthen marketing efforts, and reevaluate the best time to offer the help sessions. Evaluation information gathered during program implementation can be very useful for improvement purposes.

When evaluation is conducted at the end of the project, it is commonly called "summative evaluation." The focus is exclusively on the results of the program's impact. Summative or outcome evaluation examines whether a program or strategy is actually producing changes in the outcomes that the program is designed to address. For example, summative evaluation would answer the question of whether students were more engaged and likely to graduate as a result of the program that was implemented. It is recommended that evaluation efforts include a combination of both formative and summative evaluation. Both types have merit, and when both are utilized, a more comprehensive and informative picture will emerge.

HOW TO MEASURE

When it comes to measuring program implementation and impact, you have a choice of developing your own instruments, modifying instruments, or using standardized instruments to gather information. If you are modifying or using standardized instruments, you must attend to copyright laws, and there may be additional costs for ordering or scoring published tools.

There are many types of tools that can be used. These range from simple checklists, surveys, and complex tests to interviews, focus groups, and observation. The instrument you use should be considered in light of what is being assessed. It does not make sense to use a standardized achievement test to measure student perceptions of school climate. Be sure your evaluation tool is aligned to the purpose you want it to serve. If you want to use standardized tests, be sure to examine their technical adequacy, including measures of reliability and validity (see Box 10.3).

Box 10.3   Validity and Reliability

Reliability: The extent to which a measuring instrument produces consistent results when it is administered again under similar conditions.

Example: A reading test is reliable if students obtain similar scores when they take alternative but equivalent forms of the test within a short time span.

Validity: The degree to which an instrument measures what it is designed to measure and the degree to which it is used appropriately.

Example: A valid test of mathematics should measure mathematics knowledge or skills and should be correlated with other measures of math ability. A valid use of the test is to make inferences about knowledge of mathematics, but using the test to make inferences about reading skills would be invalid.

SOURCE: Lauer, P. A. (2004). *A policymaker's primer on education research: How to understand, evaluate, and use it.* Aurora, CO: Mid-Continent Research for Education and Learning (McREL), and Denver, CO: Education Commission of the States (ECS). Retrieved March 10, 2004, from www .ecs.org/researchprimer

CRITICAL CONSIDERATIONS IN DEFINITIONS AND CALCULATIONS

We have now come full circle. Remember, in Chapter 3 we talked about definitions of *graduation* and *dropout*. The definitions that are used affect how students are counted and the interpretation of the information that is presented. Each term carries slightly different meanings. You must be clear and specific about the outcome you are using to measure progress for enrollment outcomes. Are you interested in tracking program impact on students who complete school—even if it takes them five or more years to complete? Are you interested in tracking students who obtain General Education Development diplomas? Are you only counting students who graduate with a traditional diploma in four years? Who will be counted as a dropout? All of these kinds of questions must be carefully considered and the definitions must be clearly described in order to accurately determine program impact. Everything should be documented in print!

In addition, the type of calculation you are using for the evaluation must be clearly described. These all were referred to in Chapter 3. Table 3.3 from that chapter is reprinted here as Table 10.1 to jog your memory.

Are you interested in getting a snapshot of a group's status at a given point in time? Do you want to measure the number of students who drop out of school in a single school year, out of the total number of students who started the school year? Or do you want to measure what happens to a single group of students over a period of time? When possible, we recommend that cohort rates be used to measure program impact on student rates of dropout, school completion, or graduation. This incorporates a longitudinal approach and provides the most informative picture of what is happening with students over time.

Table 10.1 Dropout Statistics and Ways That They Might Be Used (Table 3.3)

Dropout Statistic	What It Is	Ways to Use
Cohort Rate	Rate at which students in a group (e.g., 9th graders) drop out over a certain period of time (e.g., 4 yrs)	Outcome Measure • Overall • Student subgroups
Status Rate	Rate at which students have certain characteristics at a certain point in time *Examples:* • Percentage of students who are of sophomore age who have the number of credits to be on track to graduate in another two years • Pregnant students not returning to school	Warning Measure • Identify at-risk groups needing interventions
Event Rate	Rate at which students who enter a program drop out within a single year or term	Program Evaluation • Dropout prevention program • Alternative education program

Implementation Scenario: Evaluating Effectiveness (Continuous)

One important additional piece to be addressed prior to implementation was the evaluation component. The district-level committee decided to hire a consultant from outside the school district to assist in the development of an evaluation plan and asked for a three-year commitment to conduct ongoing data collection for evaluation efforts. Committee members felt very strongly that information about implementation and preliminary outcomes should be gathered and reported on a continuous basis. The information would be reviewed three times during the academic year in conjunction with established meeting times to determine whether any changes were necessary along the way. In addition, the committee requested a final written report and presentation on an annual basis. The evaluator worked with the district-level committee as well as each of the school-level teams to identify indicators that could be measured to determine program effectiveness. The evaluator suggested collecting data using multiple methods that were relevant to the questions being asked (for example, focus groups, brief surveys, existing data already collected by the schools, such as attendance). To clarify, the evaluator was asked to provide a clear and comprehensive plan for collecting data at the district and school levels. This plan would be reviewed by the district team to determine if data were collected in the most efficient manner—keeping in mind the amount of staff and student time required—and whether the information collected would provide information that could be used to determine program effectiveness. Hiring an external evaluator proved to be very useful in providing another perspective, maintaining objectivity, and ensuring accountability.

SUMMARY

In this chapter we have highlighted the importance of evaluation. Evaluation is so important, yet so easily forgotten. Therefore, it must be embedded into any implementation or action plan. It should be noted that entire books are written on evaluation, and this chapter provided only a cursory introduction to basic yet critical concepts. You are encouraged to solicit assistance from experts in the field of research and evaluation to ensure quality. This chapter provided a discussion about *what to measure* as part of an evaluation of a program or strategy designed to prevent dropout. In sum, it is important to measure indicators associated with dropout and school completion, enrollment status, qualitative and quantitative constructs, intended and unintended consequences, as well as implementation fidelity. We also noted the difference between formative and summative evaluation methods, and the importance of both to obtaining a comprehensive picture of program implementation and impact. We ended by reviewing general methods of measurement. Critical considerations in definitions and calculations of enrollment status were also emphasized. Check your answers to the Myth or Truth? statements from the beginning of this chapter against the answers in Box 10.4. Do your explanations agree with those provided?

PUTTING IT ALL TOGETHER

This is the final chapter of the book. Throughout, we have provided information to help you learn about and understand the process of dropout. We have also

Box 10.4   Myth or Truth? Answers

1. **Myth.** Evaluating the effectiveness of your program is the least important part of your implementation plan. *Explanation:* Evaluation is a critical piece of your implementation plan and including it ensures that it will not be forgotten. (See page 193).

2. **Truth.** Evaluation can be conducted during implementation and used to help modify things along the way. *Explanation:* This type of evaluation is called formative evaluation and usually occurs at designated times during program implementation. (See page 193).

3. **Myth.** Unintended consequences that occur during the implementation process should be ignored because they are not part of your objective. *Explanation:* Documenting unintended outcomes can provide valuable insight about how modifications that might be needed to avoid undesirable or increase desirable outcomes. (See page 195).

4. **Truth.** Summative evaluation typically occurs at the end of a program and focuses on measuring impact. *Explanation:* Summative evaluation is useful for measuring program outcomes and typically summarizes program impact over a designated period of time. (See page 196).

5. **Truth.** Checklists, surveys, tests, interviews, and observations can all be used as evaluation tools. *Explanation:* All of these can be used as evaluation tools. In addition, you can develop instruments, or you can use existing instruments that have already been tried and show evidence of good reliability and validity. (See page 196).

provided tools to compile, organize, and make sense of information to address the problems you identified in your school or district. It should be clear that the intent of this journey is not just to raise rates of graduation, but to engage children and youth in school and help them graduate with the knowledge and skills necessary to successfully meet the challenges life brings after completing high school. You may have wanted more specific answers—a silver bullet that could be used to solve the dropout problem. But again, it should be clear that there is no one best way to solve the problem. Each solution must be carefully considered and developed based on information and data gathered in your setting. Although circumstances, resources, and needs vary, you have the knowledge and tools to make informed decisions about how to effectively move forward. Now it is time for you to finalize your implementation plan and put your programs and strategies into place. We hope the book has been helpful, and we appreciate your efforts to ensure successful graduation for all.

REFLECTION QUESTIONS

1. Why is evaluation such an important component of program implementation? What is your experience with evaluation? Why does it or does it not occur?

2. Think about current or potential evaluation efforts of programs designed to prevent dropout. Do they measure indicators associated with dropout and school completion as well as enrollment status? Describe.

3. Reflect on the purpose of formative and summative evaluation. Which is more important? Why?

FURTHER READING

Greene, J. (2002). *Public school graduation rates in the United States* (Civic Report 31). Davie, FL: Manhattan Institute for Policy Research.

Lauer, P. A. (2004). *A policymaker's primer on education research: How to understand, evaluate, and use it.* Aurora, CO: Mid-Continent Research for Education and Learning (McREL), and Denver, CO: Education Commission of the States (ECS). Retrieved March 10, 2004, from www.ecs.org/researchprimer

Lehr, C. A., Hansen, A., Sinclair, M. F., & Christenson, S. L. (2003). Moving beyond dropout prevention to school completion: An integrative review of data based interventions. *School Psychology Review, 32*(3), 342–364.

National Research Council and Institute of Medicine. (2002). *Community programs to promote youth development.* Committee on Community-Level Programs for Youth. J. Eccles & J. A. Gootman (Eds.). Board on Children, Youth and Families, Division of Behavioral and Social Sciences and Education. Washington DC: National Academy Press.

Patton, M. Q. (1997). *Utilization-focused evaluation* (3rd ed.). Thousand Oaks, CA: Sage.

Worthen, B. R., Sanders, J. R., & Fitzpatrick, J. L. (2004). *Program evaluation: Alternative approaches and practical guidelines* (3rd ed.). Boston: Allyn & Bacon.

TAKING ACTION

This section is for those of you who are ready to begin doing something to decrease the number of students dropping out of school. But, before interventions can be selected or designed to address dropout and school completion in your setting, you need to think about the evaluation piece of the implementation plan. It will be important to develop an evaluation plan, determine how data will be collected, and refine definitions of your outcome variables. Sample Action Tools are provided in this section.

Depending on your circumstances, there are a number of directions you can go from here. To determine what your next move should be, we recommend that you read through the statements in the left-hand column of the Guide to Action Tools, identify your most immediate needs, and then use the Action Tool listed in the right-hand column to proceed. It is important to remember that the Action Tools are sample forms that are provided to assist you in gathering and organizing data that will help you to make informed decisions about how to address dropout in your setting. The tools can be reproduced; however, they may need to be modified to meet the needs of your school or district. Be sure to check whether there are district or school policies or procedures that must be followed before proceeding with the activities you plan to carry out.

GUIDE TO ACTION TOOLS

What Do You Need to Know or Do?	Action Tool
Determine what, when, and how to measure	Action Tool 10.1: *Evaluation Plan*
Determine data collection plan	Action Tool 10.2: *Data Collection Plan*
Define your outcomes	Action Tool 10.3: *Documenting Definitions of Outcomes*

ACTION TOOL 10.1   EVALUATION PLAN

Purpose: To develop an evaluation plan for measuring program implementation and impact

Materials: Flip chart and markers

Instructions:

1. Write the categories from Action Tool 10.1: Evaluation Plan on the flip chart paper (probably one on a page). Questions you will need to answer include:

   What is the purpose of the evaluation?

   What have you considered in developing your evaluation plan (use of existing data to avoid redundancy, breadth of stakeholder input, respect for demands on student time, required resources)?

   What indicators should be measured to determine program effectiveness?

   How will data be collected? Will you collect qualitative and quantitative data?

   How will the data be analyzed? Who will analyze the data?

   What will be developed as a result of the evaluation? Will there be an evaluation report? Or presentation?

   What is the timeline for the evaluation? When will the evaluation be completed?

2. After brainstorming about the evaluation plan, discuss your ideas and document your final plan on the Action Tool.

Follow-Up:

1. Periodically review the plan to determine whether it is being followed.

2. Document any changes to the evaluation plan.

School/District _____

ACTION TOOL 10.1   EVALUATION PLAN

Title	
Overview Program Goal	
Long-Term Objectives	
Short-Term Objectives	
Evaluation Purpose	
Guidelines Considered in Developing Evaluation Plan	
Indicators of Program Effectiveness	
Data Collection Plan	
Data Analysis	
Product Development	
Timeline	

ACTION TOOL 10.2   DATA COLLECTION PLAN

Objective: To determine what and how data for the program evaluation will be collected

Instructions:

1. Identify indicators of program impact. For example, will you be measuring change in academic performance, attendance, or graduation rate? Be sure the indicators that you choose are tied to program goals and objectives.

2. Determine the data that will be collected. For example, if attendance is being measured, will you be collecting information on absences and tardies? Determine the tool that will be used to gather and measure the data.

3. Determine the population from whom the data will be gathered. Will data be gathered from students, parents, teachers, or community members?

4. Identify and document projected timeline.

Follow-Up:

1. Periodically review the data collection plan to determine whether it is being followed.

2. Document any changes to the data collection plan, and modify as needed.

School/District _____

ACTION TOOL 10.2   DATA COLLECTION PLAN

Indicator of Effectiveness	Measure or Tool	Data	Stakeholder Group	Timeline for Data Collection
Example: Participation	_Example: Days in attendance*_ _*Must define attendance_	_Example: Average daily attendance_	_Example: Students in Grade 9 (2004–2005)_	_Example: Daily for one academic year_

ACTION TOOL 10.3   DOCUMENTING DEFINITIONS OF OUTCOMES

Objective: To identify and define enrollment status outcomes that will be measured as part of the program evaluation

Instructions:

1. Brainstorm possible enrollment status outcomes such as graduation or dropout rate.

2. Define each of the outcomes you listed. Consider the complexities of the definition. For example, if you are considering tracking graduation rates, you must consider what counts as graduation, and whether the student must graduate in four, five, or more years to be counted as a graduate. Will students who obtain a nonstandard diploma be counted in the graduation rate? Must they pass a basic competency test in order to be counted as a graduate?

3. Determine the calculation procedure for each outcome you will be tracking. Weigh pros and cons of each method. What will the calculation tell you and how will it be interpreted?

4. Review the enrollment status outcomes you listed. Choose and document enrollment status outcomes that will be measured as part of the evaluation.

Follow-Up:

1. Review periodically to determine whether any changes are necessary. Is the information that is being collected what was intended? Are the data that are being tracked telling the whole story, or are there gaps that must be addressed?

2. Document any changes and make modifications as necessary.

School/District _____

ACTION TOOL 10.3   DOCUMENTING DEFINITIONS OF OUTCOMES

Outcome	Definition	Calculation

Appendix A

Directory of Action Tools

Appendix B

Selected Glossary

Adequate Yearly Progress (AYP)   Term used in the No Child Left Behind (NCLB) Act to indicate that the school or district has met its goals for improvement from one year to the next. States set their own yearly progress goals within constraints set down by NCLB.

Adult Basic Education Programs   Programs usually designed for adults and out-of-school youth ages 16 years or older who are not enrolled in secondary school and do not have a secondary school diploma or its equivalent. Goals include helping students to continue their education, become more employable, and be productive and responsible citizens.

Alternative Schools   Public elementary or secondary schools that address the needs of students who are at risk of school failure. These schools may provide a nontraditional education and tend to serve students who have special needs, including youth with unique learning interests, teenaged parents, court adjudicated youth, or youth with a history of truancy or dropout.

Certificate of Completion   Document indicating completion of a specific amount of time in school or completion of specific coursework. In some states, students may obtain certificates of completion for staying in school even though they do not meet all the course requirements. In other states, students may obtain certificates of completion for completing all of the coursework successfully but not passing an exit exam that is required. Receiving a certificate of completion generally is not viewed as being as good as receiving a standard diploma.

Charter Schools   Public schools that operate under an established charter, making them essentially a district unto themselves. Charter schools operate relatively autonomously and may be free of some of the rules and regulations governing traditional schools. Charter schools were developed to provide an innovative educational option, but they are held accountable for academic and financial results.

Check & Connect   Model designed to encourage student engagement in school and learning through relationship building, individualized interventions, promotion of problem-solving skills, and affiliation with school. The key features are carried out through an individual referred to as a *monitor* who serves as a mentor, case manager, and student advocate. The model has been used in several different applications and has shown evidence of effectiveness using an experimental research design.

Cohort   Group of individuals who enter a program at the same time. Typically, these individuals are followed over time to determine outcomes for the particular group.

Cohort Dropout Rate   Method of calculating a dropout rate in which the rate at which students in a group (e.g., ninth graders) drop out is counted over a certain period of time (e.g., four years).

Common Core of Data (CCD)   Database on public elementary and secondary education in the United States that is collected by the National Center for Education Statistics. Data are collected annually from all public schools in three categories: general descriptive data, demographic characteristics of students and staff, and fiscal data on revenues and expenditures.

Cumulative Promotion Index (CPI)   Measure developed by the Urban Institute to be consistent with No Child Left Behind yet give an approximation of the probability that a student who entered a school in Grade 9 would complete high school with a regular diploma. The formula used to calculate the CPI involves multiplication of grade-specific promotion ratios.

Diploma   Document indicating successful completion of high school. See **certificate of completion, honors diploma, special education diploma, standard diploma**.

English Language Learner   Student for whom English is not the first language and for whom educational programming needs modification because of linguistic needs.

Event Dropout Rate   Method of calculating a dropout rate in which the rate at which students who enter a program and then drop out, drop out is counted within a single year or term.

Exit Data   Type of data that the Office of Special Education Programs (OSEP) collects on students leaving school, regardless of whether they are leaving because they have successfully graduated or because they are leaving as dropouts. The exit data that OSEP collects and reports are unique from other data sets in that they summarize data for students who are ages 14 through 21, rather than looking at students at the age at which they are no longer eligible for special education services.

Five Whys   Technique for identifying the underlying cause of a problem by using a series of *why* questions.

General Education Development (GED)   Often referred to as a high school equivalency test, the GED exam allows individuals who have not graduated from high school to demonstrate they have acquired the skills and abilities generally required through completion of a high school program.

High School and Beyond   Study that surveyed a nationally representative sample of sophomores in 1980 and again in 1982. Information was collected from parents, teachers, high school transcripts, student financial aid records, and postsecondary transcripts, in addition to student questionnaires and interviews, to examine issues related to dropout, school completion, and academic success.

High-Stakes Testing   Testing that has significant consequences. Generally, in the past the term "high-stakes testing" was applied to testing that had significant consequences for the students—such as earning a high school diploma or being promoted from one grade to the next. Recently, "high-stakes testing" has also been applied to system-level testing, where consequences are applied to schools and districts that do not meet their targets for adequate yearly progress.

Honors Diploma   Document indicating successful completion of high school in a way that exceeds the traditional requirements. Generally, this means that the student successfully completed coursework that was more rigorous than the coursework required for a standard diploma. In states or districts that require that a test be passed, the honors diploma may also mean that the student passed the test at a higher than required level.

Individualized Education Program (IEP)   Individualized plan mandated by the Individuals with Disabilities Education Act (IDEA) for each student with a disability who requires special education services; the IEP is written by an IEP team and reviewed for its appropriateness. The plan must contain goals and objectives for the student's educational program and other specific information related to transition and participation in state and district assessments.

Innovation Configuration Map (ICM)   Element of the Concerns Based Adoption Model (CBAM) designed to guide the implementation of an innovation or practice.

Longitudinal Study   Study that involves collecting data and following participants over time—typically for more than one year. The purpose is to be able to draw conclusions about change over time.

Magnet School   Public elementary or secondary level school that offers a special curriculum that attracts substantial numbers of students typically from outside their attendance zone. Magnet schools have their roots in the concept of districtwide specialty schools and offer special curricula, such as math-science or performing arts programs, or varied instructional approaches.

National Center for Education Statistics (NCES)   Part of the Institute of Education Sciences of the U.S. Department of Education. It accurately describes itself on its Web site as the "primary federal entity for collecting and analyzing data that are related to education in the United States and other nations." Data cover a range of areas, including assessments, early childhood, elementary and secondary, international, library, postsecondary, and references and other. NCES regularly collects and reports on dropout and graduation data.

No Child Left Behind Act (NCLB)   Reauthorization of the Elementary and Secondary Education Act passed by the legislature in 2001 and signed by President George W. Bush in 2002. Known as No Child Left Behind, the law was groundbreaking in its requirements for disaggregated accountability and for its inclusion of graduation rates with fairly strict definitions in its accountability system.

Office of Special Education Programs (OSEP)   Office within the Office of Special Education and Rehabilitative Services that provides leadership and financial support for states and districts. The mission is to improve results for infants, toddlers, children, and youth with disabilities ages birth through 21.

Perry Preschool Project   Study that began in 1962 and, using an experimental research design, examined the effects of a high-quality preschool program on a group of children who were at high risk of school failure. Lasting program effects were identified in relation to participants' later educational achievement, economic success, and avoidance of criminal activity.

Retrospective Study   Study that involves collecting data from previous years to draw conclusions about what may be associated with, or have influenced, current status. For example, identifying students who have dropped out of school and going back into existing school records to examine their academic performance in earlier grades.

Resilient   Vulnerable children or youth who become successful as adults despite the presence of contextual factors or characteristics that place them at risk. Oftentimes protection against later dysfunction is influenced by the interplay between the characteristics of the child, the presence of an effective caregiver, and the social context.

Root Cause   Underlying cause of a problem.

Special Education Diploma   Document indicating completion of high school in a way modified for students receiving special education services. The range of modifications that are allowed varies tremendously from state to state and district to district. Generally, modifications are allowed in the coursework that must be completed. In states or districts that require that a test be passed, the special education diploma may also mean that the student passed the test at a different level, or did not have to take the test at all.

Standard Diploma   Document indicating successful completion of high school in the traditionally accepted way. Generally, this means that the student successfully completed the regular coursework indicated by the state or district as required to earn a standard diploma. In states or districts that require that a test be passed, the standard diploma may also mean that the student passed the test at the required level.

Status Dropout Rate   Method of calculating a dropout rate in which students exhibit certain characteristics related to dropping out (e.g., credits to be on track to graduate in another two years) is counted at a certain point in time.

Students With Disabilities   Students for whom a disability has been verified by an Individualized Education Program (IEP) team through an assessment and review process.

Total Quality Management (TQM)   Management approach used to implement a quality improvement program within an organization.

Appendix C

Related Links

Alliance for Excellent Education

http://www.a114ed.org
The Alliance for Excellent Education seeks to ensure that at-risk middle and high school students achieve high standards and graduate prepared for college and success in life. This organization promotes the adoption of four research-based initiatives including adolescent literacy, teacher and principal quality, college preparation, and small learning communities.

Center for Research on the Education of Students Placed at Risk (CRESPAR)

http://crespar.law.howard.edu/
CRESPAR's mission is research, development, evaluation, and dissemination of school-based and community-based programs and practices aimed at ensuring that each child reaches his or her full potential, regardless of family circumstances or other risk factors.

Center on Education Policy (CEP)

http://www.cep-dc.org/
The Center on Education Policy is a national organization that advocates for public education and more effective public schools. The organization focuses its activities in many areas, including policies on high school graduation, exit testing, and dropouts.

The Education Trust

http://www2.edtrust.org/edtrust/default
The Education Trust was established in 1990 by the American Association for Higher Education as a special project to encourage colleges and universities to support K–12 reform efforts. Since then, the Education Trust has grown into an independent nonprofit organization whose mission is to make schools and colleges work for all of the young people they serve.

National Center for Secondary Education and Transition (NCSET)

http://www.ncset.org/
NCSET seeks to create opportunities for youth with disabilities to achieve successful futures. NCSET coordinates national resources, offers technical assistance, and disseminates information in four major areas: providing access to the secondary education curriculum; ensuring positive post-school results; supporting student and family participation in decision making; and improving collaboration and system linkages.

National Center for Education Statistics (NCES)

http://nces.ed.gov/
The NCES collects and analyzes data related to education in the United States and other countries. NCES develops annual reports including *Condition of Education* and *Digest of Education Statistics*. NCES also has several survey and program areas, including High School and Beyond (a longitudinal study), and the National Assessment of Educational Progress.

National Center on Educational Outcomes (NCEO)

http://www.nceo.info
NCEO focuses on assuring the participation of students with disabilities in national and state assessments, standards-setting efforts, and graduation requirements. Topics addressed by NCEO include accommodations, accountability, alternate assessments, graduation requirements, out-of-level testing, participation, reporting, standards, and universal design.

National Dropout Prevention Center/Network (NDPC/N)

http://www.dropoutprevention.org/
NDPC/N serves as a clearinghouse for information on dropout prevention. NDCP/N conducts research, issues publications, and offers a variety of professional development activities. NDCP/N compiles a database of promising programs designed to prevent dropout that can be accessed via its Web site.

National Longitudinal Transition Study–2 (NLTS2)

http://www.nlts2.org/
NLTS2 is a study designed to document, over the next several years, the experiences of a national sample of students with disabilities as they make the transition from high school into adult roles. NLTS2 provides access to data tables online and produces reports, brochures, and newsletters of interest to many audiences on topics including high school coursework, postsecondary education and training, employment, and others.

Office of Special Education Programs (OSEP)

http://www.ed.gov/offices/OSERS/OSEP/
OSEP is a federal office that assists states and local school districts to improve results for infants, toddlers, children, and youth with disabilities. OSEP offers IDEA-authorized grants to states and other nonprofit organizations to support research, demonstrations, technical assistance and dissemination, technology, personnel development, and parent-training and information centers.

Positive Behavioral Interventions and Supports

http://www.pbis.org/
The Technical Assistance Center on Positive Behavioral Interventions and Supports (PBIS) has been established by the Office of Special Education Programs, U.S. Department of Education, to give schools capacity-building information and technical assistance for identifying, adapting, and sustaining effective schoolwide disciplinary practices.

Substance Abuse and Mental Health Services Administration (SAMHSA)

http://www.mentalhealth.samhsa.gov/
The Substance Abuse and Mental Health Services Administration (SAMHSA) is an agency of the U.S. Department of Health and Human Services (HHS) that works to support individuals who are at risk of mental health problems. Topics on this Web site include children's mental health, school violence prevention, bullying, and links to other Web sites that focus on promoting mental health.

UCLA School Mental Health Project

http://smhp.psych.ucla.edu/
The Center for Mental Health in Schools at University of California-Los Angeles strives to approach mental health and psychosocial concerns in ways that integrally connect such efforts with school reform. Its mission is to improve outcomes for young people by enhancing policies, programs, and practices relevant to mental health in schools.

What Works Clearinghouse (WWC)

http://www.w-w-c.org/
The WWC seeks to become a central, independent source of evidence of what works in education. Through Web-based databases, the WWC will provide decision makers with information based on high-quality scientific research. This information will include reviews of potentially replicable interventions to enhance student outcomes, information about evaluation studies of interventions, scientifically rigorous reviews of test instruments, and more.

Index

Page references followed by *fig* indicate illustrated figures; followed by *t* indicate a table; followed by *b* indicate a box.

**CORWIN
PRESS**

The Corwin Press logo—a raven striding across an open book—represents the union of courage and learning. Corwin Press is committed to improving education for all learners by publishing books and other professional development resources for those serving the field of K–12 education. By providing practical, hands-on materials, Corwin Press continues to carry out the promise of its motto: **"Helping Educators Do Their Work Better."**